Why Public Higher Education Should Be Free

Why Public Higher Education Should Be Free

How to Decrease Costs and Increase Quality at American Universities

ROBERT SAMUELS

RUTGERS UNIVERSITY PRESS

NEW BRUNSWICK, NEW JERSEY AND LONDON

LIBRARY OF CONGRESS CATALOGING-IN-PUBLICATION DATA

Samuels, Robert, 1961–
   Why public higher education should be free : how to decrease costs and increase quality at American universities / Robert Samuels.
      p. cm.
   Includes bibliographical references and index.
   ISBN 978–0–8135–6124–0 (hardcover : alk. paper) — ISBN 978–0–8135–6123–3
(pbk. : alk. paper) — ISBN 978–0–8135–6125–7 (e-book)
   1. Universities and colleges—United States—Finance. 2. Educational
accountability—United States. I. Title
   LB2342.S28 2013
   378.1'06—dc23   2012038527

A British Cataloging-in-Publication record for
this book is available from the British Library.

Visit our website: http://rutgerspress.rutgers.edu

Manufactured in the United States of America

CONTENTS

PREFACE

Universities are in crisis because they have lost their central identity. They were once defined by the twin goals of research and instruction, but now these two main activities are often lost in a sea of competing interests. It turns out that when a educational system or institution loses sight of its center, it spins out in many different directions, and these new interests can be very expensive and disorienting. In fact, I will argue that once a system is no longer focused on its central mission, it simultaneously increases its costs and decreases its quality. Thus, in the case of many American research universities, the more they spend, the more they often lower the quality of education and research. The explanation of this counterintuitive principle is that costs cannot be contained when there is no defining goal.

As a working definition, we can understand research to be the scientific, critical, and creative investigation of truth, and we can define instruction as the effective communication of that truth. The argument of this book, then, is that universities have lost their focus on research and instruction, and this loss of vision is the real, underlying crisis facing higher education. In other words, the movements of corporatization and privatization are only side effects of the main crisis, which is a loss of educational priorities.

Throughout this book, we will see that since there is no real institutional effort to judge and maintain quality research and instruction, false and misleading external forms of quality control are used instead, and these substitute forms end up increasing the crisis in universities. For instance, the *U.S. News & World Report* college rankings are used not only by students and parents to judge the quality of universities, but also by universities themselves to determine their own priorities. In this reverse

feedback mechanism, the system that is supposed to be judging the institution becomes the guiding force behind the institution. Making matters
worse is the fact that the chief criterion *U.S. News & World Report* uses in
its analysis of universities is their reputation, but the people who assess
an institution's reputation—administrators at other universities—have
reported that they base their judgments on past *U.S. News & World Report*
rankings.[1]

Another rating system that is equally influential for universities is that
of bond rating agencies, like Moody's. These noneducational institutions
often tell universities what they have to do in order to maintain a high
bond rating and thus receive low interest rates when they borrow money.
Like the way the International Monetary Fund tells developing nations to
privatize their economies, bond raters push universities to privatize by
increasing tuition and reducing their reliance on state funding. In addition, these raters motivate schools to cut labor costs and diversify their
revenue streams, and the result of these recommendations is that universities spend more on expensive side projects and reduce their commitment to undergraduate instruction and pure research.

Some academic readers may feel that this book unfairly criticizes professors and undermines the value of research, but the book's ultimate aim
is to correct the excesses of current university practices, which requires
not idealizing universities.[2] Although I show how national trends are shaping research universities, I do not want to remove individuals from responsibility. Thus, I both use many national statistics in this book to back up
my claims and recount personal stories in order to show how larger institutional factors change reality on the ground. Furthermore, although I rely
heavily on my knowledge of the University of California system, I match
this local knowledge with facts about national trends and statistics.

Ultimately, the goal of this book is not simply to list the problems
facing higher education; I propose concrete suggestions to make universities more just and effective. By avoiding the use of academic jargon, I
hope to reach parents and students so that I can explain how universities
have entered into a state of crisis and what can be done to pull them out
of their present predicament. As I argue throughout this work, the future
of our economy and our democracy rests on our ability to train university

students to be thoughtful participants in the production and analysis of knowledge. If our leading universities serve only to grant credentials and prestige, our society will suffer irrevocable harm. By providing a clearer understanding of how universities spend and make money, I hope to provide solutions for how we can make these important institutions not only less expensive but also more effective. Moreover, in calling to make all public higher education free, I reveal the way we can accomplish this goal by using current resources in a more effective manner.

Why Public Higher Education
Should Be Free

1

Why Tuition Goes Up and Quality Goes Down at American Research Universities

Every year, tuition at American colleges and universities goes up, but virtually no one seems to know why. In fact, the average cost of higher education in the United States increases at twice the rate of inflation, and by going up 8 percent each year, the cost of tuition doubles every nine years.[1] Meanwhile, educational institutions claim that they are losing money and that they have to rely increasingly on large lecture classes and inexpensive, untenured faculty in order to remain afloat.[2] In other words, the cost is going up, but the money spent on undergraduate education is going down. And once again, no one appears to have a coherent explanation for this state of affairs.

One possible reason for the financial difficulties of public universities and colleges is that since 1980, states have been cutting their funding for higher education.[3] In fact, if you listen to administrators at public institutions, they will tell you that if the states would just give them more money, all of their financial problems would disappear. Unfortunately, when administrators make these arguments, they are misrepresenting the situation. Although state budget cuts for higher education have forced schools to increase tuition, it is important to examine how universities and colleges spend their money.[4] To prove this point, we can simply look at the fact that even the wealthiest private universities, many with multibillion-dollar endowments, continue to increase class size, rely on graduate student instructors, and inflate tuition costs.[5] Although the number of college administrators is increasing, and that obviously helps explain the increase

1

in costs, it is only part of the problem.[6] A larger issue is how universities and colleges determine what they spend on each undergraduate student in a given year. We shall see that this calculation is the key to many different issues and helps us to explain why no matter how much these institutions charge, they never have enough money.[7]

The Department of Creative Accounting

A famous economics professor once said that statistics are like bikinis because what they reveal is seductive, but what they conceal is essential. In the case of the use of numbers by universities and colleges, this combination of seduction and concealment gets to the heart of the matter. For example, in 2009 the University of California (UC) declared that it cost close to $16,574 to educate each additional undergraduate student for a year, and since the average student was paying $5,606 and the state was chipping in $7,570, the university was losing $3,398 for each student.[8] After declaring that the state was failing to fund the full cost of educating undergraduates, the university decided in the same year that it would have to scale back enrollment by 2,300 students, raise student fees (tuition) by 42 percent, increase class size, and decrease the number of courses it offered. Once again, students would be paying more and getting less. Yet the numbers don't add up.

As Charles Schwartz, a retired physics professor from UC Berkeley, has shown, the numbers never add up in higher education because universities and colleges use a false and misleading method to determine the cost of undergraduate instruction.[9] Most American research universities calculate this important figure by taking the total cost for all undergraduate and graduate instruction, professional school education, departmental research, facilities, services, and administration, and dividing that cost by the total number of students.[10] Schwartz argues that this common method for determining cost is misguided since it assumes that all students will be taught by professors and that there is no difference between the cost of undergraduate and graduate education. In other words, when a university or state calculates how much it has to spend to educate each additional student, it includes in the costs the full salary of a professor—even though everyone knows that at research institutions, professors spend only a part of their time teaching undergraduates. According to Schwartz, parents are really paying for the cost of undergraduate instruction plus graduate instruction plus research plus administration. To be precise, undergraduates are subsidizing the cost of research and graduate education, and no one is willing to admit this fact. Moreover, although research universities often claim that their research is fully funded by external grants, we shall see that the full cost of faculty salaries and equipment, staff, and construction is not always covered by outside sources.

The reason why this calculation of how much it actually costs to educate an undergraduate is so important is that the figure determines the amount public universities charge for tuition, how much these institutions get from the state, and how these institutions can claim poverty.[11] This calculation also hides the fact that most students in higher education are now being taught by untenured faculty and graduate students, rather than by tenured professors.[12] Furthermore, this budgetary system at research universities also affects nonresearch universities and colleges, and one of the reasons why so many of the professors and administrators at these institutions were trained at research universities.[13]

As I will show in later chapters, once research becomes the priority at a college or university, the cost of administration and facilities skyrockets, and this increase is paid for in part by undergraduate tuition and state and federal taxes.[14] Undergraduate students and their parents are therefore paying for the replacement of teaching with external research and administration, and what makes this situation even more upsetting is the fact that these institutions still claim that their central mission is education. The point here is not to say that parents and taxpayers should not support university research or that university research is not important. Rather, people should know what they are paying for, and false statistics allow for a lot of hiding of the truth and mismanagement. Furthermore, research universities point out that they still cost less than private liberal arts colleges, but it is clear that these colleges—which do not have graduate students or large research facilities—base their tuition rates on what people are willing to pay and what similar schools are charging, rather than on their real costs.

A central explanation for why research universities have been able to get away with shortchanging instruction—as they pursue other areas of interest—is that there is little effective instructional quality control in higher education.[15] Not only are there no shared tests for all universities to see if students are actually learning their course material, but many universities evaluate professors based on their research and not on their teaching, which means that a professor can have a long history of being an ineffective teacher with no negative repercussions. Although some universities have used course evaluations and other monitoring methods to improve instructional quality, the combination of tenure for researchers and decreased funding for instruction has resulted in inconsistent educational quality. One solution to this problem, of course, would be to eliminate tenure for professors, but without tenure, administrators could get rid of any faculty member who has a different view from them or simply costs a lot of money.[16]

Misguided Rankings and Ratings

The question of tenure will be discussed later, but for now, we can look at how universities are rated and ranked, and why these systems of evaluation not only have no relation to the quality of undergraduate education, but also actually drive up tuition. Perhaps the most influential force shaping the priorities of higher education in America is *U.S. News & World Report*, which ranks universities, in part, on their selectivity and the average SAT scores and the high-school grades of the incoming students.[17] In other words, the universities are not ranked on what they actually do once the students get to them; instead, they are rated on who attends the schools and how many people are excluded from attending. Universities and colleges thus have a perverse incentive to recruit students so that they can reject them and thus raise the school's selectivity rating.[18]

U.S. News & World Report also rates universities and colleges based on their reputation as reported by peer institutions. This part of the ranking system has been highly controversial, but what most people fail to notice is that this reputation rating does not try to assess the quality of education.[19] In fact, none of the categories that *U.S. News & World Report* uses judge what goes on in the classroom, and the main reason for this lack of analysis is that the institutions themselves do not have any shared method for judging the quality of faculty teaching or assessing the level of student learning.[20] Since higher education institutions have not developed any accepted method of evaluating the effectiveness of undergraduate education, parents and students are forced to rely on the ranking books that the universities and colleges themselves reject.[21]

However, even if every school criticizes the validity of the *U.S. News & World Report* college rating system, these institutions still spend a great deal of money and time on trying to raise their rankings. In other words, a bad evaluation system is driving the decisions of many of our colleges and universities. For instance, in order to raise their selectivity rating, schools pour money into advertising and recruitment to make sure that many students apply. In fact, even the universities that reject the vast majority of interested students spend lavishly on trying to attract more students so they can reject more students.

Another key way that schools compete for the applications of potential students is by showing off their great athletic centers, food courts, and other extracurricular activities. Once again, due to the lack of any accepted method of evaluating student learning, colleges and universities rely on noneducational factors to attract and retain students. For example, when students and their parents go on college tours, much of the information given them relates to noneducational topics like housing, parking, dining, fraternities, athletic facilities, and entertainment options, and when college tour guides do provide information concerning educational activities, it is often false or misleading.

One important but misleading statistic that is usually discussed on tours and in college guidebooks is class size. For instance, according to the 2009 edition of *America's Best Colleges* by *U.S. & World Report*, 53 percent of the classes at Texas A&M have fewer than twenty students.[22] If we look at the university's own official listing of its classes, we find that this statistic is true, but it is based on the fact that the school offers a large number of small courses that serve very few students. Looking at the actual statistics on class size, we find that in 2007–8, there were 89 classes with 4–9 students and 596 classes with 10–19 students.[23] On the other end of the spectrum, during the same period, 452 classes had 50–99 students and 418 classes had over 100 students. The reason why these statistics are highly misleading is that they do not account for the fact that 100 classes of 500 students covers 50,000 students, while 100 classes of 5 students handles only 500 students. In other words, even with the same number of classes in both categories, only a tiny percentage of students will be able to take the small classes.

Another tricky indicator of academic quality employed by *U.S. News & World Report* and other ranking systems is the percentage of faculty who are full time. It turns out that many of the top universities report that over 90 percent of their faculty are full time, but they can make this claim only by not including graduate students and untenured instructors as faculty.[24] If these universities did count everyone who actually teaches on their campuses, the number of full-time faculty teaching undergraduate courses would be closer to 35 percent. Moreover, this statistic does not account for the facts that many professors never teach undergraduate students, and nationally, many of the classes taught by professors at research universities are graduate courses.[25] *U.S. News & World Report* also uses a statistic concerning the student-to-faculty ratio, but this number does not examine whether these faculty members actually teach undergraduate students.

This brief examination of university statistics shows that most—if not all—of the major categories are misleading, and they do not even try to account for student learning or the effectiveness of teachers. In other words, parents and students make one of the biggest and most expensive decisions of their lives based on faulty and deceptive information. As I argue throughout this book, one way to control tuition increases at universities is to get them to concentrate on their core missions of instruction and departmental research, but currently, there are very few incentives for universities to do this, and so the cost of tuition continues to rise and the quality of instruction suffers.

The Hidden Cost Driver: Room and Board

The public and the government have focused on the rising cost of tuition, but the increased costs of housing and dining have actually been the major cause of the growing expense of attending public universities and community colleges. Using national statistics, we find that in 1990–91, total tuition, fees, and room and board at public universities averaged $5,585. In 2009–10 this cost had risen to $16,712, an increase of $11,127. Meanwhile for community colleges, the total cost in 1990–91 was $3,467; in 2009–10, it was $7,703, an increase of $4,236.[26] During the same period, tuition and fees for public universities rose from $2,159 to $8,123, an increase of $5,964, while tuition and fees for community colleges went from $824 to $2,285, an increase of $1,461. This means that the biggest driver of cost increases for public higher education is room and board, but few people ever discuss this fact.

Since students and parents now expect a high level of amenities on campus, the cost of attending universities and colleges has skyrocketed. Moreover, in order to pay for the high-quality living arrangements that their customers demand, universities have gone into massive debt. Students have also taken on increased student loans to pay for this fast rise in total costs. Ironically, this push for more expensive housing and dining has resulted in a situation where funding for instruction is reduced, while spending on construction is increased.

America's Higher Education System

The rising costs at American research universities have also undermined the goal of producing more students with degrees. Increased tuition and related costs make it hard for students to graduate on time, and many students leave college because they cannot afford the constant increases. For example, if we look at California, we find that as the University of California increases tuition and limits enrollment for in-state students, more students eligible to attend UC are forced to go to community colleges instead. However, community colleges have also seen major reductions in state support, and so they have also reduced their enrollments. Thus, many students can no longer get into community colleges, and their only choice is to go to costly for-profit colleges, which often have a graduate rate below 10 percent.[27] The end result of this system is that individual students are paying more, but there are fewer graduates, and as a country, we are spending more on higher education, but we are not producing more people with degrees. In fact, in 2002 the six-year graduate rate for four-year public universities in America was 54 percent, while for community colleges it was just 20 percent.[28] As I argue at the end of this book, a key to increasing college attainment in America is to make sure that more students graduate on time. In order to accomplish this goal, we must reduce the expenses associated with public higher education. The biggest reason why students do not graduate in a timely fashion, or at all, is that they cannot afford the tuition and related costs.

Today the price for higher education keeps going up, and incomes for all but the wealthy keep going down. As a result, Americans are turning to loans and credit cards to pay for higher education. In fact, many argue that we are now entering a tuition bubble that is very similar to the housing bubble that caused the global financial meltdown. During 2012 total student loan debt surpassed $1 trillion dollars, and this figure does not include students' use of credit cards to pay for tuition and related academic expenses.[29] This high level of student debt is coming at a time when the job market is contracting, which means that many students will be unable to pay off their loans—and unlike mortgages, student loans are not forgiven when someone declares bankruptcy. College graduates will find that their life choices will be determined by their need to pay off their student loans. In many ways, we have produced a generation of indentured students.

Some critics of higher education feel that the national government is actually fueling the rise in tuition.[30] The argument is that universities know they can increase costs since students can always find a way to pay the bill, chiefly through the use of grants and guaranteed loans. The availability of these funds means that colleges and universities receive a constant flow of federal and state money, and thus the institutions have no real incentive to lower costs and decrease tuition. Moreover, due to the globalization of higher education, if fewer American students enroll, they can be replaced by international students who pay full tuition (not discounted in-state tuition) and do not receive any financial aid. However, I argue in this book that if we change how public higher education is funded in America, we can control costs by providing state and federal funding directly to the universities and colleges, rather than to the students. This structure would allow the government to require institutions to limit tuition increases, while universities would have to commit to spending a certain percentage of their funding on direct instructional activities.

Understanding Financial Aid

Related to the rise in student debt and the decrease in college graduation rates is the role played by financial aid. First of all, the use of aid makes it hard to tell how much a school actually costs: it turns out that almost everyone is paying a different price for the same education, and on average, students pay less than half of the sticker price.[31] Moreover, in the last several years, research universities and other higher education institutions have moved increasingly from need-based aid to merit-based aid. Driving this change is the competition for the students with the highest grades and test scores. In the endless race for high rankings, universities have to inflate their tuition so they can give the brightest and wealthiest students the best financial aid packages possible.[32]

In this system, lower- and middle-class students actually end up subsidizing the wealthiest students. This is because, as many studies have shown, the students who have the highest SAT scores also have the wealthiest parents. One possible explanation for this situation is that wealthy parents are better educated and can afford to send their children to better high schools. Those better high schools have more advanced placement classes and more test preparation courses, so—no matter how hard universities try to level the playing field and have a more diverse student body—economics gets in the way.[33] Of course, all of this could change if elite universities and colleges decided not to be obsessed by the test scores of their incoming students. But at this point, there are too many incentives for higher education institutions to talk about diversity while they actually pursue a narrow version of meritocracy.

As Peter Sacks has documented in *Tearing Down the Gates*, public universities across the country have been increasing the number of their wealthy students, while the number of their students from low-income families has decreased significantly. For example, in 1992 a third of the students at the University of Michigan's Ann Arbor campus were from lower-income families, but by 2002 only 13 percent of the students were eligible for Pell grants, which go to only the most disadvantaged students.[34] This precipitous loss of lower-income students also occurred at the flagship public universities of Virginia, Illinois, and Wisconsin. Between 1992 and 2002, the percentage of students receiving Pell grants at the University of Wisconsin at Madison went down by 28 percent; a decrease of 15 percent occurred at the University of Illinois Urbana-Champaign.[35] Furthermore, after reducing its reliance on state funding by rapidly increasing its tuition, the University of Virginia saw its percentage of students eligible for Pell grants drop to just 8 percent.[36]

At selective universities and colleges around the country, this conflict between the liberal desire to promote social justice and the elitist desire to have the highest rankings is evident on a daily basis. For example, each year, elite universities bring to their campuses thousands of students from poor neighborhoods in order to inspire them to apply one day to these prestigious institutions. The only problem with this "liberal" recruitment strategy is that the vast majority of these students have no chance of being accepted by universities with competitive admissions. In fact, a cynic might wonder if someone at these institutions knows that by getting these students to apply one day and then rejecting them, the universities can raise their all-important selectivity rate.

Outline of This Book

It is important to remember here that the vast majority of higher education institutions in America are not selective at all; it is only a relatively small group of colleges and universities that accept less than half of their applicants. However, these selective schools are often very large, and they produce most of the doctoral degrees in the country and set the tone for all of the other institutions of higher education. Thus, although this book does focus on research universities, many of its arguments can be applied to other types of colleges and universities.

To help explain why tuition keeps going up while universities end up spending less money on undergraduate instruction, chapter 2 offers a close analysis of how universities actually spend their money. It is surprising to realize that virtually no one has ever attempted to analyze the budgets of these important institutions. In using national statistics and detailed budgetary information from the University of California, I show how the vast majority of student tuition dollars goes to pay for expensive programs and administration that have little or no connection to undergraduate education.

After establishing in chapter 2 where the money goes at American research universities, in chapter 3 I examine why tuition increases may actually result in a decrease in instructional quality. Drawing on interviews with students and national studies of student attitudes, I will show how tuition increases motivate students to think only about gaining a future high-paying job and not about learning to be critical thinkers or involved citizens. I will also discuss the fact that some universities have realized the best way to keep students content even as the quality of their education declines is to pour money into costly recreational activities.

Chapter 4 concentrates on the effect of university finances on the faculty. I show that the vast majority of people teaching in higher education are now low-paid instructors with little or no job security. Furthermore, these teachers, who are not eligible for tenure, usually have no academic freedom, and they are judged mostly by student evaluations—a situation that sometimes forces teachers to inflate grades and teach in a defensive manner. The common view is that tuition increases are the result of high faculty salaries, but I show that in reality, tuition goes up although the use of part-time faculty and graduate students as the main labor force at research universities is driving down the cost of undergraduate instruction.

Chapter 5 examines the rising cost of administration at American universities. One of the key findings in this chapter is that as these schools increase their enrollment, they decrease the number of faculty but increase the number of administrators. In order to understand how these bureaucrats multiply like rabbits, I examine the causes of administrative bloat. I also explain that many administrators have no connection to the educational mission, and why this class of employees drives up the costs and lowers the quality of education at their institutions.

Related to the rise of the administrative class at our universities is their increased financialization. To make this point, chapter 6 argues that many of the most prestigious educational institutions are dominated by the need to borrow huge sums of money to pay for expensive noneducational construction projects and to increase the compensation of their highest paid employees. In looking at the investment strategies and funding streams of major universities, I show that much of their budget goes to risky financial investments. I also explain why so many universities lost so much money in 2008–09 and how these losses will add to the deterioration of undergraduate instruction.

Chapter 7 looks at the multiple ways research undermines undergraduate education at universities. Not only are many professors trained to concentrate on their research activities and not on their instructional duties, but research funding affects what is taught in the undergraduate classroom. In examining the research grant process, I illustrate the undermining of public education and the adoption of a profit-centered model of knowledge production. I also describe how the increase in research revenue has resulted in a decrease in spending on undergraduate instruction.

Chapter 8 examines the various ways technology raises the costs and lowers the quality of instruction at American universities. A central concern here is how students use technology to block out their teachers, while teachers use technology to block out their students. In both cases, expensive new devices undermine the quality of undergraduate education. I also analyze how universities put so much money into new technologies that they have little money left over for teachers and students.

Chapter 9 argues that the best way to improve the quality of instruction and reduce the costs at American universities is to make all public higher education free in America. In looking at the current ways our government funds universities and colleges, I argue that we may be able to eliminate tuition by simply using the current resources in a more effective manner. I also show why it is essential to stabilize the current academic labor system, and how we can reduce class sizes and improve undergraduate instruction by changing the ways we fund higher education.

In chapter 9, one of my main suggestions is to develop three types of professors: teachers, researchers, and hybrids. This new system would stop the current practice of forcing researchers into the classroom, even though such people have a long record of being ineffective teachers. Also, by creating a group of faculty who concentrate on teaching, universities could maintain and reward quality instruction. Finally, by evaluating and rewarding some faculty members, the hybrid group, based on both their teaching and research, universities could help to show the important connections that can be established between research and instruction.

The final chapter of this book looks at ways we can improve teaching and learning at American research universities. A key to this transformation is to develop an effective method of judging the quality of instruction, while making teaching a central priority at these institutions. I argue that if we want to prepare students for a multicultural democracy, we have to develop methods to teach the whole student. By presenting recent research findings in neuroscience and cognitive science, I show that our schools are now teaching to only half of the student's brain, and that we need to look at how distinct parts of our minds process information differently.

As I argue throughout this book, it turns out that the best way to control the costs of higher education is to force schools to concentrate on their core missions of instruction and research. Moreover, without strong quality-control measures, the price of higher education will continue to rise. In other words, an effective method of combating high costs and low quality is to insist on a strong system of assessing faculty teaching. However, as we shall see throughout this book, many vested interests in higher education are fighting any attempt to change the current incentive systems. The goal of this book is to fight back against these vested interests and provide an alternative view of how to lower costs and increase quality at American research universities.

2

Where the Money Goes
in Research Universities

To explain why costs go up at American research universities, this chapter will look into how these institutions spend their money. Since very few people have ever examined university budgets in a detailed and careful way, it has been easy for schools to claim that tuition never covers the true cost of education. However, if we look closely at the numbers, we shall see that there is little relation between what universities charge for tuition and what they spend on students. Moreover, even though many of the top universities have continued to increase their total revenue, most of them have used recent downturns in the economy to cut classes, eliminate teachers, increase class size, and inflate student tuition. To understand why tuition goes up and the money spent on instruction goes down, we have to look at how university budgets work.

Looking Under the Budget Hood

A Delta Cost Project report titled "Trends in College Spending: Where Does the Money Come From? Where Does It Go?" reveals that from 2002 to 2006, "total spending on education and related services declined for all types of institutions except research universities. Additionally, the share of educational spending dedicated to classroom instruction declined at all types of institutions. . . . By contrast, spending on academic support, student services, administration, and maintenance increased as a share of total educational costs over the same period."[1] In other words, as colleges and universities are spending less on instruction, they are paying more for student services, administration, and maintenance, and while the costs go up, the amount of money dedicated to improving instructional quality goes down. Although it looks like the amount of money that research universities spend on education has gone up, it is clear that this number is artificially inflated: under the category of instruction, the Delta study includes "activities directly related to instruction, including faculty salaries and benefits, office supplies, administration of academic departments, and the proportion of faculty salaries going to departmental research and public service."[2] Like most other studies of higher education, this report fails to separate direct instructional costs from other costs associated with research, administration, and public service.[3] The other parts of the budgets at public universities are the following: hospital services, 11.3 percent; auxiliary services, 8.8 percent; institutional support, 8.0 percent; academic support, 7.3 percent; public service, 4.9 percent; student services, 4.1 percent; operation and maintenance, 4.1 percent; scholarships, 3.3 percent; depreciation, 3.0 percent; and independent organizations, 0.5 percent.[4]

One thing we discover from these data is that direct expenses for instruction represent less than a quarter of the total spending by public universities. In fact, although the national statistics do not allow us to calculate the cost of undergraduate instruction, we can estimate using data from the University of California that less than a third of instructional expenses go to pay for the salaries and benefits of the faculty teaching undergraduate courses, and most of the expenses support staff and administration related to graduate education and departmental research.[5] In other words, less than 9 percent of research universities' budgets may be going to direct undergraduate instructional costs.

Calculating the Costs of Undergraduate Instruction

To gain a more accurate understanding of how much research universities spend on undergraduate education, we can look at national statistics regarding faculty salaries and how much it costs a university to staff undergraduate courses. According to a study commissioned by the American Federation of Teachers called "Reversing Course," the average salary cost per class for a tenured professor at a public research university is $20,000 (the assumption is that the average professor at such a university teaches four classes a year, earning $80,000), and it costs on average $9,000 for a full-time non-tenure-track teacher and $4,500 for a part-time instructor to teach the same course.[6] Using these averages, we can determine the annual instructional cost for each student by considering the number of classes that students take in a year, and how much each individual course costs. Since we know that only a third of undergraduate courses are now taught by professors, and the other courses are taught by untenured faculty, we can calculate the per student cost—if we know the average class size. This is the analysis that I believe no one has ever done.[7]

Looking at transcripts from several public research universities, I have determined that a common annual course load for a student at an American research university is six large classes (averaging 200 students each) and two small courses (averaging 20 students each). Using the national faculty average salary per class, and determining who actually teaches undergraduate courses (one-third professors, one-third full-time non-tenure-track faculty, and one-third part-time faculty), we find that the total average annual instructional cost per student is $1,456 (each large class costs $56 per student and each small class costs $560). In other words, in 2009 public universities charged on average $7,000 per student and got another $8,000 per student from the state, but in reality, it may have only cost them about a tenth of this amount to teach each student.[8] So where does the money go?

University officials will say that they have to pay for the classrooms and other buildings, heating, staff, equipment, and central administration, but before we get to this calculation, we should concentrate on direct instructional costs. For there is something that I have left out, and at research universities, that something is very important: the graduate student instructors. Since many large lecture classes at research universities are coupled with small sections taught by graduate students, and these sections often hold 20 students, a large class of 200 students will have ten sections, and this is where the instructional cost starts to go up. In fact, due to the need to pay graduate students to teach the small sections, large lecture classes can end up being more expensive than small classes. I estimate that the average graduate student gets $4,000 to teach a section of 20 students, so the average per student cost is $200. Thus, if an undergraduate student takes six large classes during a year, we have to add $1,200 to the annual total. In other words, the cost of having sections taught by graduate students is almost as expensive as the cost of all the other classes combined.[9] In fact, although every university says it cannot afford to have small, interactive classes because they are too expensive, in some cases, those classes may actually be cheaper than large lecture classes.

In response to this calculation, many university administrators will say that they do not have enough rooms to have many small classes. However, most of the sections taught by graduate students are in small classrooms, so this response does not ring true. The second common response from administrators is more telling: the use of sections gives graduate students jobs and teaching experience. In the crazy logic of research universities, the reason why large classes and higher tuition are needed is that there has to be some way to employ and train graduate students. Yet we should not forget that, in many fields, more than 50 percent of these graduate students will never get their degrees, and of the half who do earn doctorates, only a third of them will get tenure-track jobs.[10] In other words, most of the graduate students are really untenured faculty on short-term contracts and are being trained for jobs they will never get.

On the Use and Abuse of Grad Students

As noted above, many university administrators will respond to my calculations by saying that I need to factor in the cost of administration, utilities, and construction. However, by first concentrating on the instructional cost, I want to show that most of student tuition and state funding does not go to undergraduate education. Furthermore, it is vital to stress that although tuition has been going up at a high rate during the last thirty years, the use of large classes and nontenured faculty has actually pushed the costs of instruction down. It is therefore false for many universities to claim that they are losing money on each student; the truth is that they are often making a huge profit off of each undergraduate. What research universities do not want to disclose is that the inexpensive undergraduates are subsidizing expensive graduate students, administrators, and researchers. In fact, not only does the need to employ grad students to teach the sections attached to large lecture classes drive up the cost of undergraduate instruction, but it often costs four times more to educate a graduate student than an undergraduate student.[11] The reason for this high cost differential is that many graduate courses are small seminars taught by the highest paid professors.

Looking at these statistics, it should be obvious that one way to improve access to, and the affordability and quality of, undergraduate education at American universities is to decrease the number of graduate students and increase undergraduate enrollments. However, universities refuse to do this, in part because graduate students bring prestige to an institution. Thus, it does not matter if they never get the type of jobs for which they are being trained; what matters is that departments are ranked by the test scores and incoming grade point averages of their graduate students. Moreover, departments within the same institution jockey for position by bringing in the "best" grad students, and each professor wants to find a student to mentor and add to the prestige of his or her specialization.

Since professors often prefer to to teach small graduate seminars instead of large undergraduate courses, universities have to find people to both enroll in the small, specialized graduate seminars and teach the undergraduate courses many professors do not want to be responsible for. Grad students are the perfect solution to this problem because they have to enroll in specialized seminars to complete their doctorates, and they need to find work to support their studies. The resulting system not only drives up the costs of education, but it degrades the value of undergraduate instruction. After all, we have to ask what message it sends to students, administrators, and the general public when graduate students teach many undergraduate courses even though they do not have experience, degrees, or expertise. The message appears to be that anyone can teach undergraduate courses, and therefore there is no reason to produce doctoral degrees or hire people with doctorates in the first place. This system sounds like institutional suicide: the same institutions that produce the product (doctoral degrees) declare that these products have no value.

Staffing undergraduate courses with unprepared graduate students often leads to an inverse relationship between costs and quality at American research universities. Having graduate students teach small sections can double the cost of undergraduate education while degrading the value of doctoral degrees. Furthermore, because there are so many graduate students teaching undergraduate courses, there is no need to hire graduate students as professors once they earn their degrees. Ultimately, the use of grad students as instructors sets the bar so low for entry into the profession of university teaching that university administrators can get away with hiring uncredentialed people to teach undergraduate courses. And since there is inconsistent quality control for instruction at American universities, these schools can continue to drive down the costs and quality of undergraduate education as they move money to the more prestigious and expensive areas of graduate education and research.[12]

Other Ways of Calculating the Real Cost of Instruction

One of the results of this shifting of funds from undergraduates to graduates is that as the money spent on undergraduate education goes down, the cost of everything else goes up. To trace this movement of money, we can look at several other attempts to study the real cost of undergraduate instruction. For instance, Charles Schwartz, the retired UC Berkeley professor mentioned in the previous chapter, has examined the annual expense reports of the different UC campuses, and by taking out the cost of the graduate schools and looking only at the part (23 percent) of the professors' salaries that goes to undergraduate instruction, Schwartz found that in 2003, UC spent $497 million ($3,330 per student) on undergraduate education.[13] Schwartz then added the cost of libraries, student services, and administration dedicated to undergraduate education, as well as utilities and overhead, reaching the annual figure of $6,817 per student spent by UC. According to Schwartz's calculations, not only do the indirect costs of instruction double the total cost for each student, but even if we take into account all of those expenses, the university was still making about $10,000 on each student. It turns out that although student tuition dollars cover all of the direct and indirect costs, the state also funded each student in 2003 at a rate of $10,000 a year, and this money appears to have gone directly to administration and research.[14]

In another study, "What Does a College Degree Cost?" Nate Johnson used a similar method to look at the actual instructional costs at universities in Florida.[15] Johnson did not calculate the amount of time professors spend teaching undergraduates, but he found that the direct instructional cost per credit hour was $158, and therefore if a student graduates in four years and takes the required 120 credits, the cost per year is $4,740. Johnson then added in the cost of student services, administration, facilities, and overhead and reached a total cost of $288 per credit, almost double the instructional cost.[16]

If we now turn to private universities, we find that the costs go up because the faculty and administrators make so much more money. Yet even if we take into account these higher levels of compensation, Schwartz's analysis shows that it actually costs elite private institutions much less than they claim to educate an undergraduate student for a year. For example, looking at data provided by the Integrated Postsecondary Education Data System of the US Department of Education, Schwartz found that in 2005, when Harvard was charging students $32,000 a year, it actually cost the university closer to $18,000 to educate each student.[17] Likewise, Stanford charged $31,000, but the cost was estimated to be $16,000. If we look down Schwartz's list of comparisons between the tuition price and the actual cost at the top private universities, we find virtually the same ratio: private universities charged about twice as much as the actual cost. Although these universities claim they spend millions from their endowment funds each year to subsidize the cost of undergraduate education, in reality students are subsidizing the high cost of noneducational activities.

In response to this analysis, many people will argue that students go to prestigious institutions because they have great reputations, which allows students to go on to the best graduate schools and get the best jobs. In other words, people who attend elite institutions want the faculty to concentrate on research and raising funds because that is how universities get the best reputations. Therefore, what students are purchasing is not an education or a credential; rather, students are buying prestige and reputation. Against this argument, I claim that parents, students, and taxpayers should know where their money is going, and everyone should be concerned about the quality of undergraduate education. If students at elite institutions do not get an effective education but simply purchase prestige, our country will produce leaders, workers, and citizens who lack the basic skills and knowledge to be effective inside and outside of the workplace. However, before discussing these issues, let us return to how universities spend their money, and why their spending habits undermine their instructional mission.

Inside the Pay Raise System

Another way of examining a university's budget is to see how much employees are being paid, and how much their salaries are increasing. In order to pursue this analysis, I used a database containing the salaries of 240,000 people working in the University of California system in 2008.[18] Since I had read that most of the raises in the UC system go to people making over $200,000, I wanted to see who was making this much money, how large their raises were, and what jobs they did. First I divided these employees into six basic groups: administrators and staff, athletic coaches, business school professors, medical faculty, law professors, and academic professors (those not teaching business, medicine, or law). These six categories accounted for over 95 percent of the salaries paid to all the members of the over $200,000 club, which had a total gross pay of over $1 billion in 2008 out of a total university payroll of $9 billion. According to my analysis, the top group of my six was medical faculty: in this group, 2,296 people were making a total of $680 million in 2008. This same group in 2006 had 1,748 employees with total earnings of over $502 million. In other words, over a period of just two years, UC added 548 new people from the medical field to the over $200,000 club, and costs rose $178 million.

Another big group of earners was the administrators and staff. In 2008 there were 397 staff and administrators in the over $200,000 club, making a total of $109 million. There were only 214 members in 2006, with a collective gross pay of $58.8 million. This group and its combined salaries, then, almost doubled in just two years. The third biggest group, the academic professors outside of law, medicine, and business, also basically doubled its members and salaries: 415 academic professors in 2008 were making over $200,000, for a collective gross pay of $96.6 million; compared to 215 professors in 2006, earning $49 million together.

The same doubling applied to the business school faculty; in 2008, there were 372 of them were making more than $200,000, for a collective gross pay of $93 million; in 2006, there were 193 in this group, and their collective gross pay was $46 million. The law professors did not manage to double their earnings, but they still did well: in 2008, there were 85 of them making over $200,000, for a collective pay of $21 million; in 2006, this same group consisted of 57 employees making a collective $13 million.

I want to note that during this time, the university claimed that faculty salaries in the UC system continued to fall beneath the national average. What was really happening was that there was an incredible increase of faculty salary inequality: the rich were getting richer and the poor were staying the same.

The final group I examined was the athletic coaches. In 2008, there were 24 coaches making over $200,000, for a collective payout of $12.8 million. In 2006 this same group had only 11 members, with collective earnings of over $5 million. So athletic coaches in this highly paid category more than doubled their collective earnings in two years. What all of these statistics tell us is that UC does not just have a budget problem; it also has an out-of-control compensation problem for people at the top. Moreover, the people making over $200,000 a year—just 1.5 percent of all university employees—made 11 percent of the total compensation paid by UC, and this group increased its wealth by close to 40 percent in just two years.

Understanding the Compensation System

The overall operating budget for the UC system in 2008 was close to $19 billion, and half of this money went to compensation—a figure that does not include health benefits or pension contributions. This means that, as at other higher education institutions, most of the UC's costs go to compensation. As a result, a good way of understanding how a university functions is to see how it determines pay. Furthermore, we can read budgets as a set of implicit priorities, and as my salary analysis above shows, the UC system prioritizes professional schools and administration over undergraduate education. In fact, virtually none of the top thousand earners in the UC system have anything to do with undergraduate instruction, and so it should come as no surprise to anyone if the institution only gives lip service to making undergraduate education a priority.

Since the top administrators and faculty do not want to put money into undergraduate instruction, the result is that undergraduates pay more and end up with less. For example, in 2009 universities all over the nation decided that they could no longer pay for required writing, language, and math classes, so requirements would either have to be suspended or students would need to take these classes during the summer, online, or perhaps through for-profit extension programs.[19] In all of these scenarios, students would have to pay extra to take required classes, and they would probably receive an inferior education than if they took those classes as part of their regular course load. After all, summer classes are usually six weeks instead of sixteen (at universities using the semester system), and with a reduction in the number of weeks for each course, students would be paying more and getting less. Furthermore, universities can pay lower salaries in the summer and usually do not have to pay faculty members benefits for summer or extension work.

Athletic Budgets

One area of questionable university spending that has gotten some attention lately is the high cost of college athletics. Although most people think that university athletic departments make money, it turns out that most of them lose money, and many lose large sums that result in student tuition dollars being used to subsidize insolvent athletic departments rather than going to instruction. According to a report of the Knight Commission on Intercollegiate Athletics, "the vast majority of athletics programs reap far less money from external sources than they need to function. Virtually all universities subsidize athletics departments through general fund allocations, student fees, and state appropriations, and the NCAA [National Collegiate Athletic Association] estimates in a given year that only 20 to 30 athletics programs actually generate enough external revenue to cover operating expenses. Institutional subsidies to athletics can exceed $11 million, according to data provided by the NCAA."[20] This 2009 national survey concluded that the vast majority of university athletic programs lose money, and the biggest ones often lose the most.

Not only are these athletic departments draining money from essential programs, like research and instruction, but their expenses continue to spiral out of control: "In 2009, the National Collegiate Athletic Association published a report that found median operating spending for athletics increased 43 percent between 2004 and 2008, but median revenue generated by athletics programs grew only 33 percent over the same time period. In another telltale spending reality a few years earlier, the NCAA reported in 2005 that athletic expenses rose as much as four times faster than overall institutional spending between 2001 and 2003."[21] What is shocking about these figures is that universities are raising tuition at record rates, and part of the reason is to bail out athletic programs that are too big to fail.

According to the Knight Commission, the expenses for athletics programs break down in the following way: "Salaries and benefits, especially coaches' salaries (32% of total expenses); Tuition-driven grants-in-aid—or sports scholarships (16%); Facilities maintenance and rental (14%); Team travel, recruiting and equipment and supplies (12% combined); Fundraising costs, guaranteed payments to opponents, game-day expenses, medical costs, conducting sports camps and other miscellaneous costs (12%)."[22] As these athletic programs continue to expand and take on more functions, they cost more money and require more noneducational employees. Once again, expenses go up, and the amount of money dedicated to instruction goes down.

This connection between athletics and instruction has been discussed by Derek Bok, former president of Harvard University, in *Universities in the Marketplace*.[23] Bok argues that athletic programs and coaches are so powerful that even a university president cannot influence them.[24] This power is in part derived from the false assumption that sports teams increase enrollments and help bring in external funding.[25] The reality is that when a football or basketball team wins a championship, the university can see a slight jump in applications, but when the team loses, applications go down. Moreover, Bok questions the quality of the students who apply to an institution simply because that university has had a winning season.

Another related issue that Bok stresses is that most of the college athletes never graduate, and they end up taking places at a university that could otherwise go to students with much higher academic potential.[26] Perhaps most damaging is the fact that when universities spend big on athletics, they send the message to students that social activities are more important than learning and studying. From Bok's perspective, athletics represent the ultimate example of universities losing sight of their core mission, and these programs contribute to increased tuition as they pull money away from needed academic programs.

Changing Universities

As I have begun to show in this chapter, many of the budgetary forces at universities work to drive up tuition costs and lower educational quality, and most of the reasons for this strange combination have to do with compensation. Like the rest of America, universities have moved to a system that hands profits to a small group of individuals but spreads costs out among a wider population. Furthermore, in this system, the poor end up subsidizing the wealthy as income gets concentrated at the top. Not only do middle-class students subsidize the financial aid of the wealthiest students, but the lowest paid faculty subsidize the low workload and high pay of the top faculty, coaches, and administrators.

By understanding this budgetary system in higher education, we also begin to understand other institutions in American, like the healthcare system. Just as in the case of higher education, many of the forces in the healthcare system work to lower quality and raise costs, and in both cases, one of the keys to changing the system is to rein in the compensation of the people at the top. Of course this type of change is the hardest thing to do, because the people who make the biggest profits are the people in control.

In the next chapter, I discuss how the unequal distribution of wealth and resources at research universities affects students on a daily basis, and why students do not complain when they are paying more for less. In fact, I show that universities have found a way of keeping students happy by lowering educational standards and pouring money into extracurricular activities. This emphasis on keeping students content outside of the classroom helps to drive up costs and lower the quality of education at American universities. As strange as it may sound, a central way to fight the cost spiral is to insist on educational quality control.

3

Shortchanging Instruction at Research Universities, and Why Students Don't Complain

The previous two chapters have described how research universities have been decreasing their spending on direct instructional activities, while they increase their expenditures in other areas. In order to examine how these reductions in instructional budgets affect the education provided by these institutions, this chapter will examine the changing nature of student learning and faculty teaching and will show how the defunding of undergraduate education has resulted in a loss of educational quality. Moreover, I will argue that students at selective research universities do not complain about the shortchanging of instruction because higher education has now become mostly a means to future advancement, rather than an end in itself. And the more tuition increases, the more students make educational decisions based on their need to achieve a high-paying career to finance their skyrocketing debt.

Budget Cuts and Instruction

To understand the educational effects of reduced spending on instruction at selective research universities, it is helpful to look at recent changes at the University of California. This ten-campus system is often regarded as the world's greatest public university system, but constant state budget cuts and questionable administrative priorities have threatened to undermine the institution's core mission. Some of the ways that instruction has been downsized in the UC system are presented in Scott

Martindale's article "UCI Faculty: Quality Eroding as Class Sizes Swell." In focusing on specific classes and teachers at UC Irvine, Martindale catalogues many recent changes, both small and large: "Instead of two teaching assistants for a class of about 50 students, UC Irvine professor Mark LeVine now gets one."[1] Martindale goes on to point out that not only are there now more students per graduate student assistant, but many small, interactive classes have disappeared: "Instead of being able to lead intimate seminar classes of just a dozen or so, LeVine is under pressure to teach more large, lecture-style classes." Professors are being pushed to teach more students for less money, and students are paying more to get a worse educational experience.

In fact, the move to larger classes staffed with fewer graduate assistants means that "instead of assigning multiple, full-length research papers throughout the quarter, the history professor [LeVine] has modified class assignments for his students so they're easier and quicker to grade."[2] These changes have a profound effect on how and what students are taught, and they also diminish students' learning of important critical thinking and communication skills. According to LeVine, "we're forced to really lower our demands so that we can actually get through all the work in terms of grading."[3]

Although it is hard to come up with a single definition of instructional quality that everyone can accept, most experts agree that effective education in higher education involves teaching students how to engage in an active and critical relationship with knowledge. There is also general consensus that a high-quality education is one that gives students the opportunity—and the ability—to speak in their classes and provides them with extensive feedback on their writing. As we shall see, this type of learning and teaching is often hard to accomplish in large lecture classes that use multiple-choice exams to test students on their ability to memorize isolated bits of information. Yet one of the consequences of shortchanging instructional budgets at research universities is the move to larger classes and more standardized exams.

For LeVine, this sacrifice of educational quality defines the fundamental crisis at our nation's universities: "The whole idea in the humanities is to take seminars of 12 or 14 students, where we teach them to think critically, where we really create the scholars and doctors and lawyers. We can't do nearly as many seminars because even 20 students isn't cutting it anymore. . . . We're talking about a university that is undergoing a profound crisis."[4] Central to this professor's argument about the loss of educational quality due to budget cuts are the ideas that class size matters, and that it is very difficult to engage students in critical thinking and higher-level analysis in large lecture classes.

Universities know that small classes are often the key to effective education, but they have moved to large classes in an attempt to save money. As I pointed out in chapter 2, large classes can end up being more expensive than small classes, once you factor in the full cost of having graduate students teach the small sections attached to the large lecture classes. Unfortunately, universities rarely realize or admit this point, and Martindale tells us professors are agreeing to teach large classes now so that they can fund their graduate teaching assistants (TAs): "And tenured professors are increasingly agreeing to teach the classes. It's the only way to financially justify the continued existence of some of the university's smaller but respected academic programs and departments, professors say, and the only way to get desperately needed TAs."[5] According to this logic, professors accept the expansion of class sizes and the downgrading of educational quality because they want to provide jobs for their graduate students; in turn, the use of graduate students increases the cost of the large classes.

As this article on educational quality documents, many of these graduate students are now forced to teach more undergraduates in each section, and this increase in class size results in cutting corners and delivering an inferior education:

> Tetsuro Namba, an UC Irvine undergraduate writing TA for the past three years, has watched student-to-TA ratios go up in many academic departments. In his writing classes, capped at 21 the first quarter and 23 afterward, he's fearful of the same trend. His classes are already too large for him to be as effective as he could be, he says. "I definitely know I have shortchanged giving my students feedback just because I didn't have time," said Namba, 28, a fourth-year Ph.D. student in comparative literature. "I really wish the classes were smaller. As class sizes get bigger, the quality of education goes down because the instructor can't help them as much."[6]

The connection between budget reductions for instruction and reduced educational quality has also been described in a recent report by the Office of the President for the UC system:

- At UC Riverside, they [students] will walk onto a campus where enrollment has grown in the last three years by nearly 3,000 students—many of them the first in their families ever to attend college—while at the same time the number of faculty has been reduced by 5 percent. The result: class sizes have grown by 33 percent. Introductory physics classes that used to average 95 students have exploded in size in three years to 573 students.
- At UC Santa Cruz, students will be provided with 84 fewer course offerings and their class sizes will have spiked 33 percent. The student-faculty ratio has exploded by nearly 15 percent, and the campus lacks funding for 125 faculty FTE [full-time equivalent positions]—14 percent of its faculty positions. Yet for all the cuts, the campus still faces a daunting $38 million budget gap.
- UC Santa Barbara has over 1,000 more students than it did three years ago, but the number of staff has declined by 450 (nearly 11 percent) during that time, and the faculty has remained the same size. The results are fewer student services, larger classes and discussion sections, and reductions and eliminations in many programs.[7]

This report shows that across the UC system, classes are getting bigger, courses are being cut, the number of faculty has been reduced, and the number of students has gone up. One result of these changes is that it is taking students much longer to graduate, which means the cost of their education goes up as they stay longer on campus to get the courses they need.

Class Size Matters

It is important to stress that although the issue of class size in K–12 education has received much national media coverage and has been the subject of a great deal of political debate, very few politicians and citizens have paid attention to the effects of increased class size at research universities. According to the important research done by Lion Gardiner on the way undergraduates study and the effect that large lecture classes have on student learning, universities are now failing to perform the educational duties that society requires them to fulfill:

> Society expects college graduates to be able to think critically, solve complex problems, act in a principled manner, be dependable, read, write, and speak effectively, have respect for others, be able to adapt to change, and engage in life-long learning. But the educational experience for many college students does not meet these expectations. The studies reviewed here, taken together, consistently show that the college experience for most students comprises a loosely organized, unfocused curriculum, with undefined outcomes, classes that emphasize passive listening, lectures that transmit low-level information, and assessments of learning that frequently demand only the recall of memorized material or low-level comprehension of concepts.[8]

In his extensive analysis of numerous studies concerning the levels and kinds of student learning in large universities, Gardiner found that one of the reasons why students are not developing needed thinking and communication skills in our institutions of higher education is that the no one is really in charge of determining how and what students learn. Moreover, Gardiner stresses that large lecture classes make it very hard for students to interact with their professors and question the knowledge presented in their courses.

In Our Underachieving Colleges, Derek Bok also argues that the use of large lecture classes and multiple-choice exams prevents students from learning critical thinking and developing important verbal and written communication skills. Bok adds that although all professors say that meeting these general learning goals is essential, tenured professors often do not teach the small courses where these skills are taught and practiced.[9] And though Bok sees that large lecture classes make it hard for professors to assign extensive writing assignments and engage in valuable class dialogues, in the part of his book where he proposes solutions, he does not argue for smaller classes; instead, he proposes that professors and administrators simply change their priorities and focus on making active learning the center of all classes.[10]

One reason why class size is so important in higher education is that in large classes, students rarely have the chance to participate and ask questions, so they internalize knowledge in a passive, impersonal manner. Furthermore, large classes most often use multiple-choice exams to evaluate students, and this type of testing often prevents creative and critical thinking. And since students' grades in large lecture classes are usually based on how they score in a couple of fill-in-the-bubble exams, undergraduates are trained to see higher education as a test of rote memorization and competition for the highest individual grade.

The negative aspects of large classes often become apparent when students take a small class and demonstrate that they cannot speak or interact in an effective manner. Since their big lecture classes have rewarded them for being silent memorizers who try to figure out what the professor will put on the next test, they are unable to think independently or to examine the ideas of others critically. In fact, many teachers of small classes at large research universities find it difficult to get students to participate in class discussions, and students report that they are not comfortable developing their own arguments or research projects because they are used to simply listening to expert professors who tell them what to think and know.

Although elite research universities claim that they want to teach their students how to be independent thinkers and writers, the structure of many—if not most—classes prevents this type of education. It is also important to note that the current generation of students has grown up with the Internet and the idea that all essential information is available online; education for them is not about mastering content. Instead, they need to learn how to access, evaluate, and organize knowledge, processes that are rarely stressed in large lecture classes. In fact, the use of multiple-choice exams prevents students from developing important writing and thinking skills like the ability to sustain a complex argument. And the lack of opportunity to speak in large lecture classes means that students are not practicing vital interpersonal and communication skills that are required for work and citizenship.

Why Students May Like an Ineffective Education

In order to study how these types of classes affect student learning and motivation, I have interviewed hundreds of students at the University of California, Los Angeles (UCLA), over the past ten years. Many students report that they are quite comfortable with large lecture classes, and they like the ideas that they are anonymous and that it is up to them to go to class or not. These students feel that one of the most important things anyone can learn at a university is how to manage one's own time and priorities, so they are happy that they are not required to go to class. Some of them also report that they cannot understand the accents of many of their professors, especially in the sciences, but this does not bother them because they have learned that "you have to teach yourself" in college. According to this highly individualistic perspective, it is up to the student to sink or swim, and universities should not be held accountable for providing ineffective instruction.

In speaking with these students, I have been struck by how they tend to rationalize the shortchanging of undergraduate instruction. Many feel that they cannot expect much from a public university that is always facing budget cuts, and they also argue that they will do their real learning in graduate school. Furthermore, students in the first two years of college believe that large, impersonal lecture classes are necessary so that everyone can absorb the same basic knowledge before moving into smaller classes in their major fields. These students see general education courses and introductory classes as hoops that everyone must jump through in order to get to the next level. Yet we must question the effect of having students take large classes in their first two years. After all, if students are socialized at the start of their academic careers only to memorize information for standardized tests, how will they later develop higher-order levels of thinking?

Many of my students intend to major in the sciences or engineering, and they feel that since the type of knowledge in these fields is objective, they will not need to examine information in a critical way. Thus, they find large lecture classes and multiple-choice exams to be the best methods of instruction. Of course, the problem with this viewpoint is that it does not account for the need to become a critical and independent thinker. In fact, according to Hunter Rawlings, the use of large lecture classes in undergraduate science courses has resulted in America's failure to keep up with other developed countries:

> A substantial body of research demonstrates conclusively that the
> problem is frequently caused by poor undergraduate teaching in

physics, chemistry, biology, math, and engineering, particularly in the freshman and sophomore years. Students are consigned to large lecture courses that offer almost no engagement, no monitoring, and little support and personal attention. The combination of poor high school preparation and uninspiring freshman and sophomore pedagogy has produced a stunning dearth of science and engineering majors in the U.S. Our country now falls well behind countries like China and India in turning out graduates with strong quantitative skills.[11]

As Rawlings argues, even at selective research universities, the use of large lecture classes undermines the ability of professors to teach students in science classes in an effective manner. Not only do these large lecture classes fail to teach students important quantitative skills, but the standard teaching methods do not take into account how students actually learn.

In order to improve the quality of undergraduate instruction at American research universities, Rawlings makes the following suggestions: "We need to alter faculty incentives by making undergraduate teaching at least equal to research and graduate teaching in prestige, evaluation, and reward. And we need to do research-based teaching that takes account and advantage of the latest findings of cognitive science, which are extensive, on how students learn. In brief, they learn by doing, not by just listening to someone else; they learn by solving problems, not by passively absorbing concepts; they learn best in groups of peers working things out together."[12] In other words, even science classes have to become more interactive and collaborative, and in order to do this, universities not only have to put more money into undergraduate instruction, but they also have to change the incentive structure for professors.

The reality is that although faculty members received extensive training in graduate school on how to do research, very few studied how students learn or the best ways to teach. Instead, professors often simply learned through experience in graduate school how to teach in an effective manner, and this is just one example of how the privileging of research over instruction affects students' learning conditions. Another important factor is that many professors have very little incentive to think about how best to teach and involve students in the learning and research process because professors are hired and promoted for their research abilities, not their teaching skills. Research universities have produced some of the most important findings about how people learn and the best way to teach students today, but university professors rarely study or use this new research. Thus, even though contemporary theories of learning say that students understand and retain information best when they apply new knowledge in an interactive fashion, most large lecture classes at research universities give students very few opportunities to interact with each other, the professor, and new research. Furthermore, faculty members usually see teaching as a private and autonomous activity, so they are unlikely to see learning and teaching as forms of collaboration.

The failure to make education interactive not only results in students being bored in their classes, but it also undermines the ability of universities to motivate students to be active participants in a multicultural democracy. Although research universities often claim that a diverse student body exposes students to diverse ideas, one has to wonder what type of diversity is promoted in a large lecture class where a single professor speaks and everyone else listens. A few teachers can teach effectively in huge courses, but Rawlings argues that the experience of many students at research universities is one of alienation and fragmentation:

> Too many students are adrift in a sea of courses having little to do with one another. Many courses, even at the upper-division level, have no prerequisites, and many require no debate or public speaking or the writing of papers that receive close attention and correction. A student's curriculum is a mélange of courses drawn almost haphazardly from dozens of discrete academic departments. And there is substantial evidence that students are fleeing demanding majors in favor of easier ones that have the added lure of appearing to promise immediate access to jobs.[13]

Like so many critics of higher education, Rawlings believes that students are not getting the personal attention they need in their classes, and that too often their work receives little informative feedback. Once again, the solution to this problem is to have more small, interactive classes taught by faculty members who are committed to student learning and have an understanding of how best to teach the students of this generation.

Unfortunately, because universities feel that they must rely on large lecture classes to save money and employ graduate students, they are not motivated to make undergraduate instruction a priority.

What may change this lack of emphasis on undergraduate education at research universities is the fact that students and parents are now paying much more for tuition, and so they may demand a higher quality education. Also, new international tests are being developed that will probably show the failure of many students to learn important thinking, writing, and communication skills at US research institutions. Moreover, as the government turns its attention to accountability measures in higher education, it will become necessary for research universities to pay more attention to providing effective instruction.

Moving Online

One unintended side effect of the extensive use of large lecture classes at research universities is that this type of education can undermine the need for students to attend classes, and this may help to usher in a future age of online education.[14] After all, what is the difference between a student sitting in a large lecture class, taking notes, and a student sitting at home watching a video of the same lecture? Since in both situations, there is no interaction and very little opportunity to stop the flow of information, the use of large lecture classes paves the way for the removal of the teachers and the students from actual classrooms. In fact, a recent UCLA Humanities Task Force report included the following statement about large classes and online courses:

> Most of our GE [general education]/Lower-Division students have some experience of classes that are so big, they'd be better off watching a video performance, a close-up broadcast that is paused and (re) considered at their own pace. The bigger classes often offer no contact with the professor, in any case. Hence the number of students in the back row(s) "taking notes" on their laptops, many of whom are actually polishing their Facebook profiles. (The same students, no doubt, also wish they were at home, watching a popular BruinCast of the same information. This is an online program, in fact, that is now so popular it has caused lecture attendance to decrease!)[15]

In other words, the large lecture classes are already so impersonal, some faculty and administrators feel the courses should just be moved online. Furthermore, since many classes are being videotaped and put online, students have already stopped going to class, so there is no reason to resist putting everything on the Web. Here we see how the students' lack of interest in their classes is in part motivated by the lack of care given to teaching by some university administrators and professors.

It is surprising that a faculty group at a major university would have such a low opinion of their own instructional activities, but it is clear that major research universities apply little pressure on research professors to teach in an effective way. Nor do the universities develop strong methods for assessing student learning, continuing to rely instead on multiple-choice exams—which encourage rote memorization and limit student creativity and critical thinking.[16] Unfortunately, the main reason why these types of tests are so popular at research universities is that they are easy to grade, and they therefore cut down on the work for large classes. Standardized exams seem like the best way to test students on their knowledge, because overworked professors do not have to be burdened with the difficult task of actually judging what students think and write. It is clear that these types of exams seldom reflect the complicated nature of most fields of knowledge, but helping students to master those fields, let alone become thoughtful and critical citizens, is not a major priority at these institutions.[17]

A Short History of Educational Devolution

Most people have a different picture of higher education in America than the one given here. One reason for this is that colleges and universities have changed a great deal since the 1980s, and many parents and citizens are not aware of this transformation. In fact, what most people know about higher education is limited to the facts that college is getting more expensive, and it is harder to get into top schools than it used to be.[18] Politicians also talk only about access and affordability, and no one seems to care about the question of educational quality. Yet if we look at the major trends affecting selective American research universities, we see that these institutions continue to hire more administrators and accept more students, while the number of faculty either stays the same or goes down.

A study of national employment records in higher education shows that faculty members now make up less than 50 percent of the employees at research universities.[19]

One of the results of this mismatch between the number of students and the number of professors is that class sizes expand, and students lose the opportunity to participate in small, interactive classes.[20] Yet, as I showed in the last chapter, this reliance on large lecture classes as a way to save money is based on the faulty idea that large classes are always cheaper than small ones. If these large classes actually cost more sometimes, why do universities use them so much? The only answer I can come up with is that professors and students prefer this type of ineffective teaching.

The Academic Cease-Fire

From the professor's perspective, it is simply easier to present knowledge and not have that knowledge questioned or criticized. From the student's perspective, it is easier to just record, memorize, and then forget information; and it is much more difficult to actually think about and examine critically the knowledge presented in a class. In this type of educational cease-fire, students agree not to challenge the teacher, and the teacher agrees not to challenge the students. Everyone is happy, but is this good for democracy or even capitalism?[21]

Many critics on the Right argue that the real problem in higher education is that tenured radicals are indoctrinating students with left-wing ideologies, but what I have found is that students are very good at finding out what is going to be on the test so that they can give information back to the teacher without really thinking about it.[22] It is hard to imagine any type of indoctrination going on in this situation, because students learn how to distance themselves from their own learning experiences. What this type of system *does* breed is cynical conformity: students learn how to fit into a system in which they do not believe. Is this how we want higher education to shape our future leaders and citizens? It is important to stress that although this book concentrates on selective research universities, these schools train most of the professors and produce many of the bachelor and doctoral degrees—therefore, this relatively small group of institutions dominates higher education in America.

What Students Want

The cynical conformity of many students can be tied to the fact that they have been socialized to compete for grades during a time of high-stakes, standardized tests. Moreover, the constant increases in tuition result in higher student debt, which in turn motivates students to think of higher education as merely a means of getting a high-paying job. In fact, UCLA's Higher Education Research Institute found in its 2010 survey of freshmen across the country that "more students than ever before (72.7 percent) indicated that 'the chief benefit of college is that it increases one's earning power.'"[23] Because students are now graduating with very high levels of debt, they feel that they must use their education to ensure a healthy income—thus, this stress on financial gain makes a certain amount of sense. However, the desire for a good job not only dictates what majors students choose, but it also reshapes the meaning of college for them. For example, according to the national freshman student survey, students in the past often went to college to learn about themselves and to understand the world around them, but contemporary students say that a university education is only a way to go to graduate school or land a lucrative position.

Other national surveys have shown that while students are now receiving higher grades, they are actually doing less homework. According to an American Enterprise Institute study, "In 1961, the average full-time student at a four-year college in the United States studied about twenty-four hours per week, while his modern counterpart puts in only fourteen hours per week. Students now study less than half as much as universities claim to require."[24] This study found that students have replaced their studying time with leisure activities, so students now feel just as busy as before. However, instead of using their time studying or going to class, students are surfing the Web, joining clubs, and playing sports.[25]

One reason, then, why students at selective research universities do not complain about the poor quality of their undergraduate education is that they are having such a good time outside of their classes. Moreover, some of these universities have learned that it is often easier to please students outside rather than inside of the classroom, so schools pour money into extracurricular facilities and activities. The result is what commentators have called the "amenities race," in which universities are forced to raise tuition in order to pay for expensive noneducational activities and facilities.[26] Once again, the costs go up but the educational quality suffers.

Just as students have reduced their study time, professors have reduced the time they spend on instruction and instruction-related activities. Remarkably, the book *Academically Adrift* shows that according to national surveys, students are now spending just thirteen hours a week studying, down from twenty-five hours in 1961; meanwhile, professors spend only eleven hours a week on advising, instructional preparation, and teaching.[27] In spite of this reduction in time spent on teaching and studying, we find an increase in grades, so everybody is happy.[28]

The authors of *Academically Adrift*, Richard Arum and Josipa Roksa, argue that as universities have stressed research over instruction, professors and students have learned to game the system and work out a silent deal where professors do not demand too much, and students do not ask too many questions.[29] The authors also posit that this type of system has now spread to nonresearch universities and colleges, so that instruction has been downgraded everywhere.[30] In the case of research universities, they hypothesize that since the only way for professors to advance in their careers is to publish their research and gain external recognition, there is no reward for excellent teaching, and any time a professor spends not working on research can be seen as a loss of time.[31]

Once again, the only reason this system works is that the students don't complain, and parents and other citizens remain ignorant about the true state of instruction. However, we should not blame professors for not doing their job or being lazy; rather, the entire system motivates many professors not to value undergraduate instruction. Nor should we simply castigate students for not trying to learn, because the system does not respect critical thinking or serious study. Instead, students are rewarded for not centering their attention on the main focus of research universities, which is to engage in a critical and scientific relationship with knowledge.

To investigate what students are now learning in colleges and universities, Arum and Roksa looked at how students performed on the College Learning Assessment, an exam testing students' critical thinking ability. The authors found that after two years of higher education, 45 percent of the students in their diverse sample showed no signs of significantly improving their critical thinking, complex reasoning, or writing skills.[32] One of the main reasons for this lack of improvement is that students are doing very little reading and writing in higher education. In fact, Arum and Roksa found that half of the seniors in their survey had not written a paper of more than twenty pages in their last year of study.[33] The authors also report that in a survey of students in their first two years of college, 50 percent said they did not have to write any papers of more than twenty pages, and one-third said they had never been required to read more than forty pages a week.[34]

Arum and Roska looked at a wide range of higher education institutions, but they found similarly low requirements for reading and writing at elite universities and colleges.[35] Moreover, their survey revealed that 81 percent of the students intended to go to some type of graduate school, and 39 percent expected to earn a doctorate or other graduate degree.[36] Thus, students who report doing very little work as undergraduates still expect to reach the highest levels of education. And why shouldn't they? The grade point average of these students was 3.2, which means that they were not being penalized for their reduced work and effort.

Rate Your Professor and Your Student

One place to gain insight into what students are actually thinking about their education is to look at online ranking sites like "Rate My Professor." Although these discussion pages are often filled with comments by disgruntled students, one can detect certain patterns in the students' views. In the case of UCLA, the student association has set up its own online ranking and discussion site that is used by almost every student and that contains tens of thousands of student narratives discussing thousands of current and past UCLA faculty. Although this site does not present a scientific study of the quality of undergraduate instruction, we can look at it to see how students are experiencing their teachers and what students want out of their university education.

The most common type of comment on the UCLA professor rating site concerns what classes one should take if one wants to maintain a high grade point average. These narratives are filled with helpful advice like "Don't go to the lectures," "Study old exams," "Go to office hours," "Get the right graduate assistant," and "You only need to study for the final."[37]

We can read these comments as very pragmatic suggestions that show students helping other students to be successful, but a closer examination reveals that virtually none of the comments deal with the value of learning in itself.[38] Students appear to be focused primarily on how to get a high grade while expending the least amount of effort.[39] In other words, the flip side of research universities not putting money into undergraduate education is that students have lost almost all interest in the pursuit of knowledge. Instead, they see college as just a step they have to take in order to do the next thing, which is often to go to medical school, law school, or some other graduate school.

According to surveys of UCLA students, a majority of undergraduates plan to go to graduate or professional school, and these students know that they need to get high grades in all of their classes in order to get into the best schools.[40] Of course, many of these students have been pursuing this same strategy since elementary school, and they have been trained to focus on their grades and not let thinking or creativity get in the way. In fact, many students openly state that all they care about is getting an A, and they will do anything to attain their goal. This combination of commitment and disinterest can be highly confusing, and it is likely that our educational system has socialized students to be both cynical and competitive.

In a later chapter I will discuss what we need students to learn in higher education. Here, it is important to stress that K–12 programs like No Child Left Behind and A Race to the Top, to say nothing of the power of SAT scores in college admissions, have taught many students to simply memorize information for standardized tests. Once these young people arrive at a research university, they are quite comfortable with large lecture classes and multiple-choice exams, and they have been trained not to question their teachers or examine knowledge in a critical and creative fashion. Thus, even though most institutions of higher education claim that they value creative and critical thinking, the structure and economics of research universities work to keep students from doing anything of the sort.

It would be easy to say that universities simply do not understand the negative effects of large lecture classes and standardized tests, but when these same schools talk about their honors colleges and special programs, they reveal a very different understanding of what high-quality education looks like. For instance, many honors programs advertise that students are taught in small, interactive seminars led by expert professors. Furthermore, students are told that they will receive personal attention as they develop important critical writing, reading, and thinking skills. In other words, research universities understand what makes an effective undergraduate education, but they simply do not give most of their students access to this type of instruction.

And while universities shortchange the education of undergraduates in order to subsidize expensive graduate and research programs, as we shall see in the next chapter, these same institutions often exploit graduate students as cheap part-time labor. It does not look as if anyone wins in this system. Unfortunately, research universities are able to get away with this downgrading of instruction because students rarely complain, and the ratings of universities are seldom affected by the defunding of instruction. In fact, during the same time that the University of California reduced its per student spending on undergraduate education, the ratings of its campuses continued to climb. When I pointed this fact out to my students, many said that they did not mind if the quality of their education went down as long as the prestige of their degrees went up. I once asked my students if they would like to get As in their classes without having to ever attend or learn anything, and almost all of them said they would. Part of the reason why students no longer value learning is that universities constantly try to justify their increased costs by telling students that the only way they will make money in the future is if they have a college degree. If every part of the system tells students that education is just a means to a future job, we should hardly blame them for not caring about learning.

To counter these views of contemporary students, universities need to explain how higher education is an opportunity to become a better citizen and a more aware person, not just a wealthier worker. However, as I will discuss in the final chapters of this book, this message will not be heard if universities continue to increase their tuition and make students go into life-crippling debt. The only solution is free public higher education, and this will happen only if universities change how they do business. This transformation must begin in the ways universities treat their faculties and the value they place on instruction.

4

The Role of the Faculty
and Graduate Students
in Changing Universities

Although some people believe that universities are now controlled by lazy liberal professors who indoctrinate their students into left-wing ideologies, the reality is that professors at research universities have lost much of their power, and they now represent a small minority of the employees at these institutions. Moreover, as universities seek to cut educational costs by relying on more part-time faculty, funding is moved from undergraduate instructional budgets to other, more costly endeavors. It is true that some star professors are able to compete as free agents for high salaries and low course loads, but most professors have seen their salaries stagnate as they take on more work with less support. Thus, instead of universities being the last bastions of liberal ideology, they actually are leaders in the generation of income inequality and the movement of wealth to a small minority of star faculty and administrators.

Exploitive Institutions

The antiprogressive nature of research universities is most visible in the institutions' exploitation of graduate students and untenured faculty as cheap labor.[1] Currently, the vast majority of people teaching in higher education are instructors and graduate students with little job security and poverty-level wages. According to one study of employment patterns in higher education, in 2010 research universities produced 100,000 new doctoral degrees, but there were only 16,000 job openings for professors.[2]

Of course, not everyone receiving a PhD intends to teach, but for the last forty years, there has been an incredible mismatch between the number of doctoral degrees produced by research universities and the number of jobs available for new professors. Some people say that the solution is for schools to stop overproducing students with doctorates, but this is not a problem of overproduction.[3] There are more than enough possible positions for everyone who wants a tenured job to get one. The real problem is that universities have decided to save money by hiring graduate students and non-tenure-track faculty to do most of the teaching. In fact, one reason why graduate students cannot get tenure-track positions once they earn their doctorates is that there are so many graduate students teaching undergraduate courses. Graduate students may not know they are helping to create their own future unemployment; surely, however, their universities must know on some level that they are helping to produce more under- and unemployed academic laborers. In any case, it appears that no one knows how to stop this unjust system.[4]

Unfortunately, what we do know is that the increased reliance on part-time faculty and graduate student instructors undermines the quality of instruction at American research universities. Many untenured faculty are excellent teachers, but they are often put in situations where they cannot succeed. Many "contingent" teachers are not given offices and computers, and sometimes they are not given the time to work with students or develop their own courses. Furthermore, many graduate students are thrown into classes without receiving any training, and some are forced to teach courses outside of their own areas of research. In fact, many graduate students begin teaching undergraduate courses right after they have finished being undergraduate students, and at times they don't know much more than the students they are instructing.

Driving this system of instructional downgrading at American research universities is the idea that, as described above, research professors need graduate students to take the professors' small graduate seminars and to teach the undergraduate courses that the professors cannot or will not teach themselves. Graduate students are also employed to teach the small sections attached to large lecture classes, which poses several other instructional issues. What message does it send to students when they are taught by an expert professor in a lecture class, but a graduate student does the grading and handles the interactive aspects of the course? This splitting off of the teaching from the grading and interaction means that undergraduate students cannot question the expert professors, while the graduate students are forced to simply follow the professor's instructions. The rationale behind this system is that graduate students are being trained to teach, but in fact they are often only being trained to assist and follow orders. These teachers have little if any academic freedom, and they lack any job security; in fact, many graduate students are afraid to complain about anything because they need their professors to sign off on their dissertations and exams.

In many ways, graduate students symbolize the failures of American research universities, embodying as they do both the exploitation of part-time labor and the shortchanging of undergraduate instruction. In this strange system, the employment of graduate students to teach the small sections attached to large lecture classes drives up the cost of undergraduate instruction, while the use of small graduate seminars taught by the highest-paid faculty forces universities to use undergraduate tuition dollars to subsidize expensive graduate classes. Undergraduate students have to pay more to receive an inferior education, and graduate students discover that once they earn their doctorates, they have a very small chance of finding a tenure-track job.

Once again, while universities are often seen as the last bastions of liberalism, the truth is that these institutions have helped to usher in destructive labor practices. Through the replacement of tenured professors with non-tenure-track faculty, these schools have led the way to a new economic model that replaces job security and fair compensation with underemployment for a highly educated workforce. Moreover, research universities have created a surplus of instructors in the labor market that not only drives down wages but also increases fear due to job insecurity in a once-stable labor group. Most untenured faculty, who are now the majority of instructors, can be let go for no reason, so teachers are afraid to unionize or fight back against oppressive administrative policies. In other words, we now have a scared faculty who teach under duress and are often afraid to rock the boat or teach difficult or controversial subject matter.

This labor system for faculty is matched by a labor system for students. Not only are undergraduate students now often forced to take jobs on and off campus to pay for escalating tuition and housing costs, but many students feel they have to take on unpaid internships to give themselves a better chance at getting a job or going to a selective graduate school. As recent studies have shown, many industries now rely on the free labor of students to reduce their costs and increase their profit margins.[5] It is also important to stress that all of the work students are doing outside of the classroom can undermine their ability to learn and study, and that this is another way in which the increased costs of higher education result in a deterioration of educational quality.

As innovators of flexible labor, universities have helped to usher in what is often called global neoliberalism, and by invoking a permanent economic crisis, research universities are able to decrease their reliance on faculty with job security and benefits and increase their exploitation of teachers without tenure who are often hired at the last minute. Just as the financial crisis of 2008 brought a strong backlash against public workers with job security and benefits, neoliberal economic policies seek to concentrate wealth at the top by reducing workers' wages and benefits. Moreover, the growing online economy has copied the academic use of free labor in order to create new models of economic exploitation. The epitome of this high-tech labor system are the for-profit universities, like the University of Phoenix, which employ all of their low-paid, insecure faculty off the tenure track and use the Internet to deliver an inferior educational product that is supported through Pell grants and student loans.

Welcome to the Job Market

A central way that research universities help to create the system they sometimes condemn is through their practices for hiring new faculty.[6] For example, one of the great mysteries in higher education is why in the humanities since 1980, graduate students have been trained in fields like comparative literature, cultural studies, interdisciplinary studies, and critical theory, although there have been virtually no jobs in these fields.[7] Furthermore, the same departments that produce these new, unemployable degrees only hire in traditional areas when they are looking for new tenure-track faculty. For instance, most jobs in the field of English are still defined by historical periods—like medieval, Renaissance, and modern—and even though most new hires will migrate to different areas once they advance in their careers, hiring committees feel that they must search for people to cover the traditional undergraduate curriculum. Making this situation even more irrational is the fact that many of the new professors will eventually teach mostly graduate seminars, and so they will end up with very little connection to undergraduate education.[8]

So why do universities hire new professors to teach Modernism, but allow them to spend their time training graduate students to study film theory? Why do departments base hiring decisions on what people will teach, if the whole reward system is centered on research? There is no rational response to these questions because the system is irrational. There is a total disconnect between the graduate and undergraduate curriculum; in addition, the hiring practices of research universities are in part psychological exercises in which opposing factions conduct turf wars, fighting for resources and prestige.[9] Due to the job crisis in many academic fields, the number of qualified applications for a single position has skyrocketed, and it can be argued that there is simply no rational way of comparing candidates. For instance, some jobs attract over a thousand qualified applicants from all over the country. How in the world can a hiring committee in this situation make a reasonable choice? It is impossible, and so they enter into the strange world of applicants' comparative prestige and future potential.[10]

Hiring Prestige

Since so many people with PhDs are now pursing a small number of tenure-track jobs at research universities, departments are able to pick and choose among the "best" people, but this competition is often centered on an irrational determination of future research value. It turns out that prestige is proven either by an already solid reputation or by the future potential of a brand-new degree. In fact, one of the cruelest truths about this type of job market is that if you do not get a job while you are completing or just about to complete your doctoral degree, you have very little chance of ever getting a good job. According to the psychological logic of hiring committees, people who have been "on the market" for a few years must be inferior because if they were great, someone else would have swooped them up already.

Getting an academic job, then, is a lot like trying to find a spouse: if you are forty and unmarried, people often think that there must be something wrong with you. Of course this type of unspoken thinking ignores the reality that there are thousands of people looking and only hundreds of jobs.

The reason why people outside of the academic world should know about this system is that it helps to explain why elite research universities spend so much to hire new professors, and why these new hires often do not help to improve undergraduate education. The new hire is like a stock option, in the sense that the hiring committee is betting on getting someone relatively cheap who will increase in value because everyone else will want to hire that person in the future.[11] After all, this is not about having well-known professors who will attract potential undergraduate students who want to study with, for example, great literary theorists: high-school seniors applying to college know nothing about the academic star system. So in the case of the humanities and the social sciences, the point must be that stars attract the best graduate students. This is true, but remember those graduate students will often be used as cheap labor, and after they get their degrees, most of them will not be able to get a good job because there are only so many potential stars.

It used to be that if you got your doctoral degree from an Ivy League institution, you were virtually guaranteed a tenured position. Now universities are full of faculty with Ivy League doctorates who have no chance at tenure. One of the main reasons for this situation is that certain classes—or even whole fields—are considered not to be part of the prestige and research economy, so departments hire only people outside of the tenure system to cover these classes. Courses like writing, foreign languages, and introductory math are staffed by untenured faculty because the faculty who teach these subjects mostly teach undergraduate students. It does not matter if the faculty have written important books or even bring in outside grant money, what matters is that they are attached to the undergraduate teaching mission—which means they are not worthy of a secure position or good pay. In this system, a small minority of wealthy star faculty are rewarded for concentrating on research, while the people who are teaching the undergraduate courses are often punished with lifetime job insecurity and low compensation.

Inside the Star System

To gain a better idea of how this system of inequality at elite research universities functions, we can look at some recent developments at New York University. In order to increase its status and rankings, this private university decided to go on a hiring binge for star professors. David Kirp reports that one of the results of this process was that the university spent much more money but had fewer people to teach its courses. In turn, the school had to hire many untenured faculty and graduate students at low salaries and with high workloads in order to staff required classes. Kirp writes that over 70 percent of the undergraduate courses at New York Universtiy are now taught by non-tenure-track faculty and graduate students, while star faculty renegotiate their salaries to make sure that they earn more and teach less.[12]

This academic star system has been replicated around the country at selective research universities, and Kirp argues that in this "free agency" system, many faculty are no longer loyal to their institutions. In the University of California system, for example, over 80 percent of the professors now have what they call "off-scale salaries," which often means that they have privately negotiated special deals for higher pay and reduced workloads.[13] In this type of structure, star professors seek outside offers from competing universities and then threaten to leave if their department does not renegotiate their deals. One result of this system was that in 2009, universities across the nation were forced to lay off untenured instructors who teach the majority of required classes.[14] Most universities blamed a reduction of state funds or a loss of endowment funds in the recession for the need to lay off these teachers, but part of the reason why some schools had run out of money was that the full professors had been receiving huge raises and decreased workloads, and there were no funds left to pay for "temporary" instructors.

The global fiscal meltdown of 2008–09 increased the problems with the academic star system. Institutions whose endowments went down and whose state funding was cut had to reduce their spending by eliminating the positions of untenured faculty. However, many universities soon realized that if they let their untenured teachers go, they would have to cancel most of their undergraduate courses.[15] These schools also had to face the fact that it was virtually impossible to get rid of tenured faculty, and so the only thing they could do was to increase the sizes of classes, reduce the number of course offerings, and reduce the number of sections attached to large lecture classes. In other terms, the quality of education would have to suffer because schools had locked up much of their money in expensive deals with star faculty and administrators. Furthermore, since the majority of undergraduate classes are now taught by faculty outside of the tenure system, these teachers are the first to go whenever there is the need to reduce a budget, and the paradox of this system is that the people teaching required courses are considered temporary, while the star faculty, who are often ready to jump to another university, are considered permanent.

It is important to stress various people's reasons for not wanting to rock the boat. Since almost everyone wants to be a star, the nonstar professors often accept the star economy because they believe that they will someday enter into the world of the highly compensated.[16] In turn the star professors who have negotiated private deals with administrators often form a covert alliance with them, which means that the faculty are less likely to use their academic freedom to criticize the administration. Moreover, these private deals circumvent the peer review process, which means that the foundation of shared governance and academic democracy is undermined: in other words, some faculty have been bought and no longer play their role in setting the agenda for universities. In the next chapter I will examine the role of the new administrative class in increasing costs and reducing educational quality, but here I want to focus on how the academic star system has helped to undermine the entire profession.

How Professors Destroyed Their Own Profession

One of the important side effects of the ability of star faculty to renegotiate their salaries and workloads is the growing need to hire more untenured faculty at increased levels of economic exploitation.[17] Although many people have written about the growing use of contingent and adjunct teachers, very few have written about the causes of this system.[18] Most of the critics who do cover this issue tend to blame cost-cutting administrators for the use and abuse of untenured faculty, but these accounts do not show

how some professors have had a leading role in the destruction of their own profession.[19]

Unlike many other professions, higher education has done virtually nothing to protect the degrees and the credentials one needs in order to enter into the profession. What few people have noticed is that by using graduate students to teach undergraduate courses, professors have told administrators that one does not need a doctorate to teach on the college level. In other words, departments have unintentionally sent out the message that there is no reason to hire people with PhDs. Thus, the door has been opened for the hiring of part-time faculty and non-tenure-track teachers. And another message has gone out: some professors and departments do not really value undergraduate education. Moreover, the need to have more graduate instructors to teach undergraduate courses has often pushed programs to recruit an increased number of graduate students, even when the departments know that there will be no jobs for these graduate students after they earn their degrees. Whether they have chosen to do so or have been forced into it, departments have devalued their own product (PhDs) and have lowered the bar for entry into the profession so much that cost-cutting administrators can feel free to have noncredentialed people teach courses.[20]

Many untenured faculty are great teachers, but they are usually not given the tools to succeed. For instance, many instructors are not hired until the last minute, and they are so worried about not being rehired that they teach in a defensive manner. In addition, they usually lack any academic freedom or institutional support. The fact that tenured professors have helped to create and maintain this highly exploitive system should make one question the need for tenure. After all, if tenure is supposed to protect academic freedom in the classroom, and most people now teaching have neither tenure nor academic freedom, the foundation for tenure is undermined. Yet I am not arguing here that we should simply get rid of tenure. Without it, there would be no possible way of blocking cost-cutting administrators. What we need instead is a way of giving job security and fair compensation to instructors, and I will discuss this solution in the final chapters of this book. For now, I want to turn to how globalization is actually feeding the exploitive labor system in higher education and undermining America's future economic competitiveness.

Graduate Students and Globalization

Just as research universities often end up supporting an educational system that exploits graduate students and non-tenure-track faculty, the Commision on the Future of Graduate Education promotes a model for graduate education that will only add to the unjust employment system in higher education. Although the commission's 2010 report argues that the federal government needs to pour billions of dollars into graduate programs to make America more competitive in the new global knowledge economy, this extensive study ignores most of the basic problems that I have been discussing in the employment practices at American research universities.

The report begins with an interesting analysis of the current state of the global economy:

> The manufacturing economy was built on the shoulders of citizens who had a high school education and who could rest assured that their livelihoods would be secure until they retired. But times have changed, and the knowledge economy, which is based on creating, evaluating, and trading knowledge and information, has arrived. Predictions are that the U.S. economy will become bifurcated, with one sector of the workforce performing services that cannot easily be exported, such as hospitality services, construction, car repair, and healthcare, while the other sector will perform work in the knowledge industries. The production of goods and services such as automobiles, electronic goods, and clothing is likely to continue to take place in other countries where there are lower labor costs and workers with lower literacy levels and educational attainment.[21]

According to this analysis, jobs not requiring graduate education will be mostly shipped overseas (except for construction and car repair), so the only jobs we will have left in the United States are ones that require a master's degree (nursing, social work, teaching) or a doctoral or professional degree (science, law, medicine). In other words, not only do we need to produce more undergraduate degrees, but we will also have to increase the number of graduate degrees.

This report predicts an increase in the demand for college and university faculty, but it assumes that most of these future jobs will be off of the tenure track: "The projection for postsecondary teachers is mixed. This occupation is projected to grow over the next 10 years due to two factors. First, an increase in student enrollment in higher education will reflect the projected population increases of 18–24 year olds, with increased numbers of students in colleges requiring increased numbers of instructors. Second, the expected retirement of current faculty hired in the 1960s and 1970s will produce openings. However, much of this growth will not be in full-time academic positions, which are a shrinking proportion of the academic workforce, but rather in adjunct or nontenured positions."[22] The report's authors never criticize or challenge this shift from tenured to untenured positions; instead, it is accepted as inevitable. Furthermore, although this national report affirms that doctoral students in the humanities and social sciences have very little chance of getting a tenure-track job when they graduate, the authors recommend that universities simply mentor students so they will accept jobs outside of the academy: "Little is known about students' willingness to invest in the type and length of training for the doctorate if a tenure-track position is not the light at the end of the tunnel. If the tenure-track position remains the desired goal, students and faculty may have to adjust their mindset to a more complex landscape."[23] According to the logic of this report, if doctoral students anticipate getting jobs in the profession for which they are being trained, they should change their expectations and realize that their education does not fulfill its intended mission. This position is similar to saying to medical students that even though you have spent the last several years studying to be a doctor, and you have gone into massive debt as a result, you should consider another occupation. Moreover, why should graduate programs continue to accept more doctoral students if the people in charge of these programs know that there are no good jobs for the students once they graduate? One response to this question that I have discussed throughout this book is that professors need graduate students to take their graduate seminars and to teach undergraduate courses, even though universities do not know what to do with these doctoral students once they graduate. The solution that many universities are now turning to is the same one that is being pushed by this report: motivate students to use their academic degrees to pursue nonacademic jobs.

Unfortunately, the report combines its recommendation that universities encourage graduate students to consider jobs outside of higher education with statistics showing that most graduate students in the humanities and social sciences do not get jobs outside of academia: "According to one estimate about half of the doctoral recipients with post-graduation employment commitments obtained jobs outside of the academy, but the percentages vary widely by field (85% from engineering, 66% from physical sciences, 38% from social sciences, and 14% from humanities)."[24] Although it is clear that many graduate students in the sciences gain training and education that prepares them for specific nonacademic jobs, it is unclear what graduate training in the humanities and social sciences trains students for besides being professors in the humanities and social sciences.

Before further analyzing the future of graduate education in the humanities and the future of American professors, we should realize that for the sciences and related fields, the majority of students earning doctorates at American universities are from other countries. Thus, our most successful programs might be actually training our competition in the global knowledge market: "In 1977, 82% of doctoral degrees awarded in the U.S. were granted to U.S. citizens, but by 2007 this figure had fallen to 57%. In engineering only 29% of doctoral degrees went to citizens (down from 56% in 1977), and the percentage today in the physical sciences is 43% (down from 76% in 1977)."[25] It may seem xenophobic to be disturbed by the fact that most of the US doctorates in the sciences and engineering go to students who are not citizens. But that fact should make us question why one of the central proposals of this report is to increase federal funding for foreign students: "Because there is a need for U.S. graduate schools to continue to attract the best and brightest students from around the world, universities could apply up to 20% of the total fellowship funding to support international students."[26] According to this logic, we need more federal funding for graduate programs because we are losing our competitive edge in the global knowledge economy, so the solution is to pour more federal money into the training of foreign graduate students.

The secret truth at the heart of this report is that graduate education in America is not always driven by the goal of improving our job market or educating students; instead, graduate education is sometimes about generating prestige and profit. Thus, graduate programs in the sciences need to continue to recruit students from outside of the United States because these students have higher test scores, and therefore they help to push up the rankings of the graduate departments. Moreover, these foreign grad students provide cheap labor to staff science labs at American universities, and many of these students pay full tuition and do not receive financial aid.

While graduate students in the sciences are helping to produce important knowledge and research, graduate students in the humanities and social sciences serve to staff high-enrollment undergraduate courses. As explained above, one of the effects of this system is that once these students earn their doctorates they cannot get good jobs in academia because so many courses are already being taught by other graduate students. The report glosses over this problem in the following way: "This shift has resulted in a change in the overall mix in the proportion of instructional staff that are in full-time tenure-track positions. The move to using adjuncts, graduate students, and non-tenured lecturers to teach the increasing college population is also reflected in a move to hire new faculty off the tenure track. . . . For many doctoral students, however, explicitly preparing for a career in the business, government, or non-profit realm will be the most prudent path to take."[27] The argument here appears to be that we need more teachers in higher education, but since we cannot stop exploiting them by hiring them off the tenure track or by turning them into inexpensive graduate student instructors, all we can do is to tell them to lower their expectations and take a job unrelated to their particular training once they finally earn their doctorates.

One of the great concerns of the report is that not only are our universities accepting too few grad students, but the ones who are accepted often fail to get their degrees: "Despite the rigorous selection processes used for graduate admissions and the high achievement level of those pursuing a graduate degree, some estimates indicate that the attrition rate in doctoral education is in the range of 40% to 50%."[28] Of course, one reason why so many students drop out and why it takes others so long to graduate is that since they are forced to teach so many courses, they do not have enough time to work on their dissertations. The result of this system is that after ten years of study, many graduate students end up with nothing but a huge amount of debt: "But even if more loan dollars were to become available, it is not clear that increased student debt would solve the problem. Current data indicate that master's degree graduates who have debt carry a cumulative debt load of $51,950 at graduation on average, and doctoral students who have borrowed report an even steeper debt burden of $77,580. Clearly these debt loads may have a chilling effect on aspirations for graduate school and may impact completion rates themselves."[29] The increase in undergraduate student debt has received a lot of attention, but many people do not know about the massive loans accumulated by graduate students. Not only are these students starting their careers with huge amounts of debt, but their employment prospects have been greatly reduced by the overreliance on graduate students and untenured faculty to teach the majority of undergraduate courses. This problem forces us to return to the theme of how the exploitive economic system of the university mirrors the systems outside of the university. It is clearly false that universities are either isolated ivory towers or the last bastions of liberalism.

How Everyone Loses in the Academic Labor System

The unprogressive nature of the academic employment system has meant that a few top professors do very well and almost everyone else suffers. Not only are the majority of the faculty now working without job security or academic freedom, but they are often excluded from participating in their faculty senates or departmental committees. A side effect of this exclusion of most faculty members from shared governance is that the people doing most of the teaching are not able to participate in the decisions regarding what is taught or other educational matters. Another is that the dwindling number of professors with tenure have to take on more of such work. Many professors, then, are not avoiding teaching because they do not like it, but because they do not have time for it: they are being told to do many other things instead, like sitting on committees and hiring new contingent teachers and graduate students who go through the revolving door to other jobs after only a few years.

As I will argue in the final chapter, one of the solutions to this problem is to simply get rid of the system in which graduate students teach the small sections attached to large lecture classes and handle other course assignments. Instead, we need to fully fund graduate students' education and transform the majority of courses into small seminars taught by full-time faculty with some type of job security. This may seem like a very expensive transformation, but I will show how we can actually reduce costs by increasing the number of undergraduate students and decreasing the level of unemployable PhD students. In other words, we need to find a way to improve the labor system in higher education as we contain costs and enhance educational quality. Much of this can be accomplished by changing how universities spend their money. Unfortunately, as I will discuss in the next chapter, the growing number of university administrators are not only taking up a larger percentage of university budgets, but they are also contributing to the continual decline of instructional quality while increasing the level of labor exploitation.

5

The Rise of the Administrative Class

In the summer of 2000, I was sitting at a bargaining table with ten university administrators, discussing the different ways of assessing the quality of teachers in the University of California system. I started to get frustrated because the conversation was going nowhere, but then I realized that no one on the other side of the table had ever taught or had studied teaching in their life. It was at this point that I began to discover the true absurdity of a research university: most of the people employed by these important higher education institutions have no background or training in education. Instead of universities being run by the faculty, these schools have become giant corporations controlled by competing interests, and although instruction is one of the institutions' many concerns, it rarely becomes the main priority of administrators, lawyers, human resource experts, and other staff. Moreover, as the number of tenured faculty relative to the number of students goes down, the number of administrators always seems to increase. This chapter is dedicated to understanding why this class of employees keeps expanding and how this expansion undermines undergraduate education.

Growth by Committee

The secret history of the research university is that as these institutions have expanded, professors end up losing their power to the administrative class. For instance, professors used to advise their students about what courses to take, but now there is a whole group of professional advisors who perform this task. Also at one time, faculty raised funds, negotiated contracts, and put together budgets, yet all of these tasks are now performed by highly paid professional administrators. Likewise, faculty used to sit on committees that would oversee the development of the curriculum and make sure that faculty were covering what they were supposed to teach, whereas now it is usually a dean of instruction who watches over these matters. In other words, as faculty lose control, administrators move in and take charge, and this change ends up costing universities more money and giving more power to people who are not primarily educators.[1] I once got to see how this whole process works firsthand when I was teaching at a University of California campus. This story begins with the creation of a task force to study the effectiveness of general education courses that were also supposed to teach writing and communication skills. Early on, the task force discovered that due to the use of large lecture classes and inexperienced graduate student teachers, many of the writing-intensive courses were offering no writing at all, and some of the courses that did require graded writing were taught by teachers who had no training or background in writing. Also, due to the large size of most of the classes, it was impossible for students to work on their verbal skills, since there was rarely an opportunity for students to speak in class. The task force then cut to the heart of the educational problems of large research universities: the classes were too big to perform their intended function, and the people teaching the lecture classes and sections had no expertise in the required subject matter.

After performing this important function of examining the quality of instruction, the task force came up with one central solution, which was to hire an administrator to make sure that people were teaching what they were supposed to teach. Therefore, instead of requiring smaller, interactive classes or faculty trained in the teaching of writing, the committee decided that it was best to pay someone a lot of money to make sure that people at least appeared to be doing the right thing. This process reveals one way that the administrative class grows as undergraduate instruction suffers.[2]

No One Is in Charge

Perhaps the biggest reason why administrators keep increasing as instruction is shortchanged is that universities have taken on so many different missions that there really is no one in charge—no one who has a finger on the whole enterprise. For instance, many universities now run medical centers, research laboratories, venture capital enterprises, and community service centers, and although all of these activities have some connection to education, they have virtually no direct relation to undergraduate instruction. In fact, as I pointed out in chapter 2, the undergraduate instructional budget at research universities often makes up less than 10 percent of total operating costs, so education is not a major priority. However, while the role of the core mission continues to shrink, we find that the role of administrators continues to grow. After all, you need administrators and staff to run medical centers, regulate research centers, oversee venture capital enterprises, and administer community service programs. In fact, you need administrators to watch over the other administrators and staff to collect the information so that this can happen. And of course you need computer staff to compile the data to give to the staff, to allow them to give the first group of administrators the information they need to watch over the second group. Once you get to this level of complication, you need a whole other set of people to see if everyone is following state and federal guidelines, and the expansion continues to infinity. There is virtually nothing stopping the spread of this group of highly compensated employees, and the only people who could rein in administrative bloat are the administrators, who—not surprisingly—don't seem highly motivated to reduce their own population.[3]

According to the Delta national study of university budgets, "over the 1998 to 2008 period, the share of instruction spending declined against increased spending for academic support (libraries and computing), institutional support (administration), and student services."[4] In other words, universities are spending less money on instruction but more money on noninstructional activities, and once again, we see how the increase in costs can result in a decrease in educational quality. Moreover, the Delta report stresses that it is not increasing faculty salaries that are driving the increase in university budgets: "The common myth that spending on faculty is responsible for continuing cost escalation is not true. In fact, in public institutions, spending for instruction saw the greatest relative declines during the 2003–2008 period, with absolute cuts in this category during the first part of this period in all public sectors."[5] Due in part to the growing reliance on untenured faculty members, the cost of instruction has been driven down, while the cost of everything else has escalated.

The Goldwater Institute has accounted for this movement of university funding from instruction to administration in the following manner: "Between 1993 and 2007, the number of full-time administrators per 100 students at America's leading universities grew by 39 percent, while the number of employees engaged in teaching, research or service only grew by 18 percent. Inflation-adjusted spending on administration per student increased by 61 percent during the same period, while instructional spending per student rose 39 percent."[6] Once again, noninstructional costs keep outpacing instructional costs, and the result is that the educational mission is downsized as every other part of universities continues to grow. To illustrate this point, the Goldwater report adds: "Arizona State University, for example, increased the number of administrators per 100 students by 94 percent during this period while actually reducing the number of employees engaged in instruction, research and service by 2 percent. Nearly half of all full-time employees at Arizona State University are administrators." Although this report has a very broad definition of administrators, it is clear that schools like Arizona State University are combining a lowering of instructional costs with an increase in noninstructional expenditures.

One possible explanation for this shift of funds from instruction to administration is that as states reduce their support for universities, these schools have to seek out other revenue streams. Thus, the authors of a recent American Association of University Professors report observe:

As these institutions try to increase fund-raising, external grant, auxiliary unit (e.g., residence halls and food services), and technology transfer revenues, they increase positions in these realms. Moreover, universities too often invest in ill-fated, costly ventures with little or no input from those who do the work of the academy. Certainly, other factors, such as increased state regulation and accountability demands, also contribute to climbing administrative costs. The key point, though, is that efforts to generate monies from external grants, fundraising, auxiliary services, and other nonacademic activities increases [sic] administrative costs and can never fully replace state support for the core academic functions of the academy.[7]

In their search for more funding, universities constantly pursue costly ventures that rarely pay off, and the result is that instructional budgets are robbed, as administrators take on more responsibilities and earn more money.

An example of how this expansion of administration can hurt education at public universities can be found in the area of fundraising. Public research universities now spend a great deal of money and time trying to increase their endowments, but the money that they raise rarely ends up in the classroom. Most people who donate to schools give the money for very particular purposes that rarely concern the educational mission—wealthy donors tend to give money to get their names on new buildings or to help finance the football team. And universities themselves restrict where the money from other donors can go. The common practice is for most donations to go to the general endowment, from which each year a certain percentage—usually around 5 percent—is released for general purposes. From the administrative perspective, this means that 95 percent of the endowment is "restricted" and thus cannot be used to fund more teachers or reduce the cost of tuition. Moreover, when schools suffer a major loss of funds, as happened after the fiscal crisis of 2008, they claim that they cannot use more of their endowment to help control tuition increases or protect the quality of education.

If we step back and look at this endowment system, we see that it both helps to increase the number of staff and administrators and draws money away from instruction as it pushes up the cost of tuition. Some people would note that a university with a $5 billion endowment is able to use $250 million for general purposes, but we must investigate how much it costs to raise this money, and how schools actually spend their endowment funds. It turns out that since so much of the endowment money is given for particular purposes, administrators are able to argue that they cannot use this source of revenue to control costs or increase instructional spending. Moreover, due to the lack of transparency in university budgets, it is hard to tell where endowment money actually ends up or whether the amount of money donated for a particular project ever fully covers that project's cost. What we can tell is that fundraising is a major contributor to the growth of the administrative class.

Who Are the Administrators?

One way of understanding how the population of administrators is expanding is to compare the rate of growth of different employee categories. For example, according to a 2008 UCLA Faculty Association report, "over the past decade, the numbers of Administrators in the UC almost doubled, while the number of faculty increased by 25%. The sharpest growth took place among Executives and Senior Managers: 114%. Because Administrators command high salaries and benefits, any increase in their number higher than the expected growth rate for the University results in high costs: rough estimates of the costs of carrying extra administrators at UC range around $800 million."[8] Not only, then, is the number of administrators growing at a much higher rate than the number of faculty, but these administrators have higher salaries. Therefore, when their numbers increase, their percentage of the overall budget increases even more. As I showed in my analysis of the UC budget in chapter 2, in 2006 there were 214 staff and administrators making over $200,000 each, for a collective gross pay of $58.8 million. Two years later, there were 397 staff administrators making over $200,000, and their total compensation was $109 million. In other words, in just two years, the number and cost of high-earning administrators almost doubled.

It is clear that one of the driving forces for the increase in student tuition is this rise of the administrative class, but we are still left with the question of how and why this group of employees continues to expand. To answer this question, Charles Schwartz, the retired UC Berkeley physics professor, examined employment data covering a ten-year period (1997–2007), and he discovered some remarkable facts. He compared the rate of administrative growth in the UC system to the rate of growth at other universities: "In 2006, in public universities across the country, 49% of the professional full-time employees, excluding the medical school, were faculty members. At UC that percentage was about 25%."[9] The increase in the number and percentage of administrators really took off in the ten years between 1997 and 2007: "In 1997, there were almost 2 faculty to every Executive and Senior Manager; by 2007 the numbers are nearly the same for both groups, while the Middle Manager group steadily grows higher."[10] These statistics show that management is growing at double the rate of the faculty, and so although UC enrolled more students during this period, it had fewer people to teach them, but more people to manage the teachers and run the business.

In looking at what particular job categories grew the most, Schwartz discovered that computer analysts and budget analysts had the highest rates of growth: "Computer Programming & Analysis—from 2,084 to 4,325 for an increase of 108% and Administrative, Budget/Personnel Analysis from 4,692 to 10,793 for an increase of 130%."[11] It is interesting to note that this growing class of administrators includes people whose primary job is to produce and analyze data for other administrators. In fact, Schwartz argues that one explanation of how administrators multiply like rabbits is because top managers increase their power and control by hiring more people to work under them: "Administrators and executives tend to make work for each other, and that is because executives prefer to have subordinates rather than rivals, they create and perpetuate bureaucracies in which power is defined by the number of subordinates."[12] It is not so much that the work of top administrators continues to grow; rather, administrators' power and influence grows when they hire more people to work for them.

Of course, it is easy to reply that universities have become so complex and diversified that one needs an army of bureaucrats to make sure that everyone is following state and federal laws and all books are being balanced. Schwartz's response is to show that although the total number of employees increased by 38 percent during the period 1997–2007, the number of middle managers increased by over 100 percent. It is hard to imagine why the university needed so many more analysts to provide information and data to upper managers when the rest of the staff was not growing as rapidly.

Understanding the Administrative Class

As Benjamin Ginsberg argues in *The Fall of the Faculty*, a major side effect of the increase of administrators at American universities is that schools are taken over by an invisible class of employees who often have no background in education.[13] Students and their parents may still feel that it is the faculty who run the show, but professors have actually lost much of their power as their numbers have shrunk, and as the proportion of faculty members with tenure or any other type of job security has decreased sharply. To prove this point concerning the increase in administrative power and the decrease in faculty control, Ginsberg cites case after case in which administrators went against the will of the faculty. This includes secret deals with tobacco companies that prohibited faculty from discussing or publishing their research, funding for expensive athletic facilities without any faculty input, presidents refusing to step down after the faculty voted to oust them, and administrators declaring a financial emergency to shut down entire academic programs.[14] In fact, since the global fiscal meltdown of 2008, many administrators have been able to increase their power by declaring "states of emergency," which allow them to break contracts, lay off tenured faculty, and restructure academic units. In this version of the shock doctrine, crisis is used as an opportunity to impose administrative plans that are hard to enact in normal times. Like countries that declare military rule in a state of emergency, administrators have used downturns in the economy to justify removing the faculty from the decision-making process.

Ginsberg adds that this type of administrative power grab often takes the benign form of setting up commissions and study groups, and we can examine this claim by looking at the University of California's Commission on the Future of the University, which was set up to deal with the fiscal crisis of 2008–9. The first thing to point out about this commission was that it was organized by administrators, and very few members of it were faculty members. Instead, the university decided to staff the commission chiefly with administrators, business people, and outside leaders who were flown in from all over the state for several rounds of meetings in order to determine how the university could survive in a time of diminished state support. Of course, the first irony of this project was that so much money was spent on trying to figure out how to save money.

If we look at the commission's final report, we see that not all of this time and money was well spent, because few people on the commission had any understanding about how the university actually works. The first sign of this lack of understanding comes in the report's opening pages, where the commission discusses the dire economic situation of the UC system: "state funding has not kept pace with inflation and enrollment growth, particularly over the last decade. Since 1990–91, average inflation-adjusted state support for educating UC students declined 54 percent. Student fee increases have addressed only about two-fifths (40%) of this decrease. Other actions to reduce costs have resulted in reduction in staff and instructional offerings, faculty and staff salary lags and reductions in funding for instructional equipment, library materials, and facilities maintenance."[15] The goal of this opening is to let people know that the university is in a crisis, and the sole cause of the problem is the reduction in state funding and not anything to do with the way the administration spends its money. Although we should not underestimate the problems caused by state budget cuts, it is important to look at what is not included in this summary of the university's financial and educational health.

The first thing to stress is that in this section, and indeed throughout the entire report, there is virtually no mention of educational quality or how the loss of state funds is affecting what students learn or how teachers teach. There is also very little mention of the high cost of increased administration or the expenses related to subsidizing money-losing athletic programs. Instead, the report focuses on how the university can become more efficient and raise more revenue. Of course, this focus is not surprising since many of the people on the commission were from the world of business; they naturally adopted a business-oriented approach.

Even though it is clear that most universities are not businesses and are not run like corporations, administrators and outside advisors often act as if these schools are educational factories, and their main product is academic degrees. This business administrative logic can be seen in the first commission's recommendation: "Implementing formal programs that encourage and facilitate a shorter time to degree, such as 'packaged' options for three-year degrees with pathways that make full use of advanced placement credits and summer terms. Such pathways could include joint bachelor's/ master's degree programs."[16] According to this factory logic, the best way to produce more products (degrees) at the same cost is to simply decrease the time it takes to make each product. No one is concerned here about educational quality or whether students will be learning enough; instead, the idea is to find ways to move them more quickly through the system.

This lack of concern for educational quality is coupled with a major misunderstanding of the economics of universities. We find a prime example of this conflict between economic theories and educational realities in the following passage: "Admittedly, the education of upper-division students is more expensive because of smaller classes and necessary specialization and facilities. As implemented, the resource consequences must be monitored. From an aggregate perspective, however, transfer students require only two years of UC resources in order to graduate with a UC bachelor's degree. Serving transfer students increases the number of degrees the UC can confer with any given level of instructional resources."[17] The first part of this argument acknowledges that the courses taught in the first two years are relatively inexpensive due to the size of the classes, but the second part of the argument insists that transfer students would save money because it takes them only two years to graduate. This claim makes no sense because the effect of increasing the ratio of less expensive lower-division students to more expensive upper-division students would be that the university would have to spend more money on average to educate each student. Furthermore, many of these transfer students would not graduate on time, so it is false to claim that they would all get their degrees with only two years of education at the university.

With their obsession about moving more people through the system more quickly, these administrators and business consultants fail to grasp the basic economics of the system with which they are dealing. For example, we know that it costs much more to educate each graduate student in comparison to each undergraduate. But the commission argued that the university should increase the number of graduate students in relation to undergraduates: "To be excellent in national and global terms, however, the proportion of graduate enrollments relative to undergraduate enrollment must be adequate to support the research and instructional mission."[18] It is unclear whether this statement means that the university needs graduate students to teach undergraduates, or the university needs to increase its number of graduate students to retain its prestige and support its research mission.

At one point, the commission does note that the proposed increase in graduate students would require a decrease in support for undergraduate students: "The education of graduate students is more expensive than undergraduate students, both in instructional costs and student financial support. Therefore, under current and the baseline fiscal projections, funding for graduate enrollment growth would require that campuses reduce undergraduate enrollment."[19] Given this awareness of the high cost of graduate education, it becomes hard to rationalize the following recommendation of the commission: "Recognizing UC's role in the Master Plan as the state's primary research and doctoral-granting institution, the Commission recommends that the University increase the proportion of graduate enrollments from 22 percent of total enrollments to 26 percent by 2020–21, with individual targets set by each campus."[20] From a strictly budgetary perspective, it makes no sense to replace the profit-generating undergraduate students with costly graduate students. In fact, due to the often low levels of support for graduate students in the UC system, it would be much more cost-effective and fair if the university reduced the number of graduate students and increased their funding.

It should be clear at this point that the commission's recommendations do not fit together and suffer from the group's lack of understanding how money actually flows at research universities. Because the commission is not looking at the ways the different parts of the university budget interact, many of the proposed ways of saving money will actually cost the university more in the long run. For example, the call to derive $250 million from self-supporting programs, like extension courses, fails to recognize the fact these programs often appear to turn a profit because they are not charged their fair share for buildings, administration, staff, benefits, and maintenance. In other words, self-sustaining units are not actually self-sustaining, and they rely on using UC facilities and faculty even though they claim to be separate and private. Moreover, as the report posits, most of the profits of these self-sustaining units come from one source: "Current UC self-supporting programs generate about $100 million annually, about $25 million per year above program costs. However, most of that revenue comes from the high-cost, self-supporting executive MBA programs. To date, most other self-supporting programs are relatively small and generate modest amounts above programs costs."[21] Unless the university wants to shut down most of the privatized programs and increase the production of executive MBAs, the commission's recommendation will only increase costs and move money away from needed instructional programs.

Another example of the failure of business-oriented administrators to grasp the basic economics of the institution they are trying to reorganize can be found in the area of private fundraising. As I pointed out above, the solution of simply trying to increase the endowment to fund the university's operations may not result in any increased funding for the core mission of the institution. In fact, the commission partially recognizes this problem in the following passage: "The University's history of fundraising, however, is marked by a high level of restriction on the funds raised. Approximately 95 percent of UC's overall endowment payout is restricted, contrasted with 80 percent for most public institutions and 55 percent for private institutions. Only two percent of all gift support in recent years is unrestricted, even less for endowment. To put this in context, of the $1.3 billion in funds raised in FY 2008–09, just over $25 million could be characterized as unrestricted."[22] Not only are most of these endowment funds dedicated to specific projects, but it is clear that they often fail to cover the full costs of the programs and positions they support.

After running through the different ways to raise and save money, the commission finally turns to tuition as the possible solution to many of the university's fiscal problems: "Although tuition cannot singlehandedly solve UC's budgetary challenges, it is a key component of any funding strategy and one of the only revenue sources that UC can effect to replace other funding shortfalls. There still exists substantial headroom on each campus for across-the-board tuition increases without impacting enrollments."[23] In other words, the system's campuses can raise tuition and still attract a high number of students, so each campus should be able to set its own price. Once again, we see how when all else fails, administrators always find a rationalization for increasing tuition and making students pay more for less.

At the end of this commission's final report, we find a series of contingency plans that can be used if the university continues to lose money. Using the shock doctrine and the fundamental essence of crisis capitalism, the business-administrative commission makes a host of problematic suggestions that could be implanted in the case of a financial emergency:

Curtail student enrollment, potentially falling short of achieving the Master Plan ratios recommended by the Commission (see

Recommendation 5) and restricting access at both the undergraduate (freshmen and transfers) and graduate levels. Re-examine UC's
financial aid strategies, also recommended by the Commission (see
Recommendation 7), including reducing the portion of new undergraduate tuition revenue that is set aside (currently 33%) to fund
financial aid for needy students. Raise or eliminate the systemwide
limit on the proportion of nonresident undergraduate students
admitted and enrolled (the Commission recommends a 10 percent systemwide cap in Recommendation 8). Substantially increase
tuition and fees, including charging differential tuition by campus
(see Recommendation 17), as part of a broad-based program to
sustain the University. Downsize the University's faculty and staff
workforce, including limiting the replacement of faculty lost due to
retirements, terminations, and other separations.[24]

These strategies would have the effect of reducing the number of students
and faculty, while increasing tuition and reducing financial aid. Of course,
there is no mention here of decreasing the number or cost of administrators or of protecting the quality of instruction. Rather, in the administrator's perfect world, there would be fewer professors and students and more
administrators to run things.

Secret Deals for the Administrative Class

Universities not only waste money on administrative bloat, but they often
justify their wasteful spending by arguing that they must pay administrators and bureaucrats top dollars in order to retain them: if they do not
spend lavishly on these employees, other schools will steal them away. This
type of thinking has led UC and other universities to engage in activities
that border on the illegal. In fact, in 2006 a series of stories appeared in
the media documenting how the UC regents were granting lavish compensation packages to top administrators, and how many of the perks going
along with the high salaries were not being reported. After several articles
in the *San Francisco Chronicle* and a legislative hearing, it became clear
that the university was constantly breaking its own rules in order to give
administrators hidden compensation. According to one *Chronicle* article,

"University auditors told the UC Board of Regents they had found that 143 exceptions to the university's compensation policies had been made to give extra pay or benefits to 113 senior managers."[25] However, these secret deals and broken rules were only the tip of the iceberg. It turned out that for years, the university had been hiding its compensations deals from the public by only reporting some of the money that top executives and employees were getting. Thus, even though UC is a public institution, it had failed to fully disclose many of its decisions and policies.

In 2006 a state audit of the university found hundreds of examples of misspent public funds and secret deals for top administrators. Here are some highlights from the *San Francisco Chronicle*'s reporting on the auditor's findings:

- Thirty-nine people getting extra vacation.
- Fourteen senior managers receiving honoraria from the university—$200 to $13,000—despite a policy against it.
- Fourteen senior managers receiving incentive payments in violation of UC policy or not approved by the regents. Some are continuing awards of up to 15 percent of base salary.
- Thirteen housing-related payments that violated policies.
- Six sabbaticals granted to employees who didn't qualify for them or who were paid more than policy allowed.
- Eleven stipends that either were not approved or were extended without approval.
- Eleven cases of extra severance pay promised.[26]

One of the things to note about all of these examples is that they concern secret deals of extra compensation; in other words, none of this money is listed in the public records of the employee's salary.

To see how wasteful a university can be, it is helpful to look at several other costly forms of secret spending that draw money away from vital instructional activities as they raise the compensation of the wealthiest employees. For instance, the state audit of the UC system found the following:

> The *Chronicle* reported the university's settlement pact with former UC Davis Vice Chancellor Celeste Rose. Under that agreement, UC

Davis agreed to give Rose $50,000 and keep her on the payroll for another two years, at $205,000 a year—without requiring her to do any work—in exchange for her promise to drop any claims of race or gender discrimination against the university. The audit revealed that one executive who was paid well to move within California was Mitchell Creem, associate vice chancellor and CFO [chief financial officer] of medical sciences at UCLA. Creem received a $150,000 relocation allowance and 11 weeks of temporary housing—well beyond the limit of 30 days. The regents were never told.

In another case, Thomas Jackiewicz, associate vice chancellor in the UC San Diego medical school, received a $40,000 "relocation incentive" even though he lived within California, which violates policy and was not approved by the regents. He also was promised a severance package that exceeded university limits.[27]

These examples show what happens when the administrative class takes over a university, and they are able to reward each other without any level of public scrutiny.

In one of the most shocking findings of the auditor's report, we find the following statement: "The University of California said it struck at least 700 separation agreements with employees over the past five years—worth about $23 million."[28] To understand how a university can spend $23 million on people leaving, we can look at the following examples:

When UC Berkeley Associate Athletic Director Mark Stephens was passed over for a promotion at Cal last year, the university promised to keep him on the payroll, giving him $183,000 over three years while letting him take a full-time job somewhere else. . . .

In 2002, the UC Berkeley athletic department forced administrator Kevin Reneau to step down but agreed to keep him on the payroll for 2 1/2 years at $86,000 per year so he could reach retirement age and his family could qualify for health care benefits.[29]

These are just a few examples of the hundreds of cases of secret wasteful spending, and they tell us that when a university says it has no money to pay for things like teachers and smaller classes, the reason for the institution's lack of money may be due to the fact that it has been taken over by some administrative employees who do not view quality education as their top priority.

In fact, as I will show in the next chapter, the administrative focus on money rather than instruction is taken to new heights when we examine how universities invest their money. On a fundamental level, we will see how research universities are being taken over by people who treat these institutions as if they are investment banks. We will also see that the more universities finance their growth through debt, the more they become beholden to bond raters and other nonacademic powers. In the case of the wealthiest universities in the United States, we will discover that when their high-risk bets do not pay off, students and parents are left paying more and getting less.

6

The University as Hedge Fund

In the winter of 2009, some of the most prestigious private and public research universities in the United States announced that they would have to scale back class offerings, increase class sizes, limit the hiring of new faculty, and restructure academic programs. The main reason for these changes was that the schools had lost billions of dollars in their endowments due to the global financial meltdown. In other words, the wealthiest educational institutions in the world were now saying that they were poor, and the main reason for their poverty was that they had invested and lost a large part of their money in the stock market and other financial vehicles. According to the official story coming out of the media centers of these multibillion-dollar institutions, everybody including them lost money at the end of 2008 and the start of 2009, so all of their employees would have to tighten their belts and reduce their spending. However, just like major Wall Street firms, universities continued to give giant compensation packages to the people who had been personally responsible for losing billions of dollars. In fact, I know of no investment specialist or executive from any elite university who was punished or fired for losing sums of money that dwarfed the entire budget of most universities and colleges. This is not only a story of bad fiscal management; more profoundly, it is a story about the inverted priorities of many research universities.

Losing Billions and No One Knows

My interest in the way universities invest and spend their money was piqued in May 2009, when I discovered that the University of California (UC) system had lost over $23 billion dollars during a fifteen-month period. I knew that other schools had lost a lot of money, but I had no idea that one institution could lose so much, and I was concerned that no one was talking about these losses. All I heard was that the state of California was going to cut the UC budget by $812 million, which is a giant number but hardly compares to $23 billion. When I asked faculty and administrators why no one was talking about this larger number, they all said either that they did not know about these losses or that everyone was losing money.

About the time that I discovered how much UC had lost in its pension fund and endowment investments, I came across a podcast by the head of Yale University's investment group, David Swensen.[1] In this short broadcast, one of the pioneers of new university investment strategies discussed how he changed the whole financial method of Yale's investments and how his high-return method was virtually risk-free. Like a used car salesman, Swensen was laughing at the institutions that failed to follow his method and bring in unbelievable rates of return, and there was a certain amount of scorn in his voice for the stodgy old investors who did not move their money into real estate and several classes of exotic financial securities. It is true that the universities that did follow Swensen's lead showed a very high rate of return for their investments for a few years, but once the markets turned sour, these schools were left holding billions of dollars in nonliquid assets and devalued real estate. In fact, like so many other financial investors, the wealthiest institutions did not know how to value much of their portfolios. However, the story goes much deeper and gets much worse.

The Failure of the Well-Endowed

One thing to keep in mind is that private universities and colleges often spend between 3 percent and 5 percent of their endowments each year in order to subsidize student tuition and to pay for their expenses. While public universities rely on the state to help support their undergraduate and graduate teaching and research missions, private institutions turn to their investments to supplement their spending. Both types of schools spend large amounts of money recruiting new donors and managing their money, and this system of funding appears to work until universities' investments lose money. Then everything is turned upside down. After all, what do you do when you have become dependent on a certain source of money, and the funds from that source are reduced by 30–40 percent?

It is also important to note that since these wealthy institutions use their endowment money to subsidize their financial aid packages, when the endowment plummets, they are forced to cut aid.[2] Furthermore, due to the fact that schools want to still entice the best students to come, they have to reduce their need-based financial aid while maintaining their merit-based aid. Thus, when high-risk investments stop paying off, students with less money have less chance of attending elite institutions, while the wealthiest students have a greater chance. Also, as I mentioned above, the way that schools deal with the loss of revenue is to reduce class offerings and increase class size, which means that risky investment strategies end up causing a further deterioration of educational quality.

In this boom-and-bust system, when schools bring in a lot of money through their investments, they spend lavishly on star faculty and highly compensated administrators, and these large compensation packages end up draining money from the core mission of instruction. Thus, even a good investment run can actually hurt instruction. However, as I am beginning to show here, a bad return on investments can also hurt the educational mission. In this situation, the only people who gain are the ones with the high salaries, who continue to earn big bucks whether their institution is losing or gaining money. In fact, after the UC system lost its billions, the university president, Mark Yudof, announced that in order to stop other schools from stealing top UC faculty and administrators, it would be necessary to raise the pay and the perks of star faculty and administrators.[3]

Is Harvard Poor?

Harvard, the wealthiest university in the world, lost at least $8 billion of its endowment during the financial meltdown, and—like many other institutions—this rich school began to plead poverty. Due to its losses,

Harvard said, it would not only have to consider curtailing an ambitious financial aid program targeted at students whose parents made less than $60,000 a year, but many classroom activities would have to be scaled back.[4] Interestingly, like Cornell and other Ivy League universities, Harvard had followed Yale's supposedly low-risk, high-return strategy, so much of its losses were due to the move to a more volatile investment portfolio. In this case, when Yale lost, Harvard—with its bigger endowment—lost even more. And what has really upset some people is that money managers at Harvard and other elite institutions sometimes make over $20 million a year each in bonuses—which they get to keep even when their risky gambles end up losing billions of dollars. The administrators who hire and manage the money managers also get to keep their inflated salaries. There seems to be an inevitable push toward privatizing the profits of these schools, while everyone else gets stuck paying for the losses.

According to a Tellus Institute report titled "Educational Endowments and the Financial Crisis," Harvard, Dartmouth, MIT, Boston College, Boston University, and Brandeis University all embarked on the same high-risk investment strategy that has resulted in reduced endowments, budget cuts, delayed construction projects, and job eliminations.[5] Like other higher education institutions across the nation, these universities all followed the model of Swensen, Yale's investment chief, by relying on alternative assets such as commodities, real estate, and private equity. It turns out that a driving force behind this move to risky investments is the role of trustees and regents with conflicting business interests. According to a *Bloomberg* article on the Tellus report, "the investment committee at Dartmouth, in Hanover, New Hampshire, included more than six trustees whose firms oversaw more than $100 million in investments for its fund over the last five years."[6] In other words, the people overseeing the finances of universities are often working in the financial industries, and thus they have a large conflict of interest. For example, the trustees with large holdings in real estate were motivated to push universities to invest in this area even when the real estate market started to tank.

Not only are large endowments and pension funds plagued by conflicts of interest, but—as the Tellus Institute report explains—these huge pots of money also contributed to the global financial meltdown: "By engaging in speculative trading tactics, using exotic derivatives, deploying leverage, and investing in opaque, illiquid, over-crowded asset classes such as commodities, hedge funds and private equity, endowments played a role in magnifying certain systemic risks in the capital markets. Illiquidity in particular forced endowments to sell what few liquid holdings they had into tumbling markets, magnifying volatile price declines even further. The widespread use of borrowed money amplified endowment losses just as it had magnified gains in the past."[7] One reason why these wealthy universities have taken on so much debt is that as they started to lose at the global speculative casino, they decided to double their highly leveraged investments.

One might ask why would these universities, full of the most brilliant people in the world, make such bad financial decisions. One response in the Tellus study is that "college governing boards have failed to guarantee strong oversight of the Endowment Model by relying heavily upon trustees and committee members drawn from business and financial services, many from the alternative investment industry."[8] The people who are charged with overseeing these schools now come from the world of business and high finance, and they are willing to involve these institutions in complicated financial transactions that other staff, the faculty, and students do not understand. It is also important to stress that not only do some trustees and regents profit from having universities invest in real estate, derivatives, private equity, hedge funds, and construction, but the people who handle the universities' investments also often take home huge compensation packages, as mentioned above: "In 2003, in-house bond traders David Mittelman and Maurice Samuels [at Harvard] each earned more than $35 million in compensation, while Meyer himself pulled home a cool $6.9 million. The bonuses drew the ire of alumni and Harvard President Larry Summers, so Meyer reluctantly instituted a cap on bonuses the following year. Nevertheless, even after the cap Mittelman and Samuels again earned bonuses of more than $25 million in 2004, and Meyer's pay increased to more than $7 million."[9] Universities say that they have to pay these huge compensation packages in order to attract the best and brightest investors, but one has to wonder why these traders did not have to give back their bonuses after so many of their deals had gone bad.

In the tradition of privatizing profits and socializing the losses, Harvard's recent investment history stands out as an extreme case. Not only were traders given hundreds of millions of dollars in bonuses leading up to the financial meltdown, but after the fall, whole communities saw their jobs and tax base disappear. For instance, before it lost so much money in its investments, Harvard was planning an extensive expansion in the Allston area:

> The amended "institutional master plan," which Harvard has regularly filed with the city of Boston, projected a 50-year expansion of its physical presence in Allston, unfolding in two phases, each involving the construction of 4 to 5 million square feet of space for the sciences, the arts, several professional schools, including the Harvard School of Public Health, the Graduate School of Education, and the Business School, as well as undergraduate and graduate housing, and other academic uses. At the time the university explained that "Harvard's Allston Initiative is expected to generate approximately 14,000 to 15,000 jobs over the next 50 years, with about 5,000 jobs created in the first 20-year phase. The construction of academic projects in Allston is expected to generate an average of 500 to 600 construction jobs per year for each of the estimated 50 years of development."[10]

Unfortunately, to help finance this project, Harvard made several risky deals and investments, and when these tanked, the university halted its expansion.

As the Tellus study affirms, the result of Harvard's putting the brakes on the Allston project will be devastating:

> We estimate that a one-year delay in moving forward with the initial Phase IA projects would result in lost direct earnings of more than $85 million and a total economic impact for the region of approximately $275 million. A two-year delay would result in lost short-term earnings estimated at more than $170 million, and a total economic impact of approximately $550 million. With a three-year delay, the figures increase to more than $270 million in lost earnings and a total regional economic impact of more than $860 million over the first three years. These impacts are driven solely by the forgone earnings of construction workers and permanent employees; they do not include the impacts of the lost procurement spending for

construction materials and equipment that would have occurred in the region. Our estimates are therefore conservative in nature.[11]

When Harvard and other universities tie their financial fate to volatile investments, there can be a devastating effect on the surrounding communities.

Perhaps the biggest way that university investments can hurt neighboring communities is through taxes. Since universities have a special tax-exempt status, their presence undermines the local tax base. For example, the universities examined by the Tellus Institute all have extensive real estate holdings but pay very little property taxes:

> The six colleges we have studied are all among the largest land and property owners in their respective communities. MIT occupies 168 acres in the dense city of Cambridge. Even though about 72 percent of its total assessed property value of almost $3.5 billion is tax exempt, MIT has nevertheless been the largest property taxpayer in Cambridge for more than a decade. Harvard also ranks as one of the top five taxpayers to Cambridge, though the vast majority of its holdings are also tax exempt. Among the many tax-exempt educational and medical institutions in Boston, Boston University is the largest property owner with an assessed value of almost $2.4 billion, 89 percent of which, valued at more than $2.1 billion, is tax-exempt. Virtually all of Boston College's $576 million of property in Boston is tax-exempt. And in the rural town of Hanover, New Hampshire, Dartmouth College's tax-exempt property has an assessed value of almost $1.3 billion, which is equivalent to 58 percent of the total assessed value of taxable property in the entire town.[12]

Since these schools are paying very little taxes for their huge property holdings, the local governments are suffering huge revenue losses.

The Tellus Institute report also notes that the compensation policies of these universities heighten social inequality:

> Even when the Endowment Model "works" best by generating excess returns, the rewards given to top management during the flush years have distorted pay scales on campus and within higher education more broadly. And because these schools are among the very largest employers in their communities, magnification of social

inequality in campus pay scales shapes wider increases in social inequality throughout their regional economies. The exorbitant pay these senior administrators have received is passed along in the form of higher prices within their local economies, raising the cost of living in ways that magnify the effects of widening pay differentials even more acutely.[13]

It turns out that since universities generate a high level of income inequality, they end up driving up housing costs and causing people to turn to risky loans in order to pay for housing needs. In fact, these universities were major contributors to the cause of the global financial meltdown in 2008.

To highlight this connection between income inequality and the risky investment strategies of wealthy universities, the Tellus study examines the growing wage inequality at these institutions:

> The average unionized staff member at these schools earned roughly $27,400 in 2000 while the average full professor's salary was about $109,000 (4 times the unionized staff figure), while the average president's salary was $346,000 (more than 12.5 times the figure for union members). Given the effects of compounding of even modest differences in pay increases, the pay gaps widen over the decade. By 2008 the average union staff member earned about $37,000, while the average professor earned $155,000 (more than 4 times the unionized staff figure), and the average president's salary grew to $561,000 (now more than 15 times the union figure).[14]

Although we often think that universities are generators of social equality, we see here that instead they often magnify economic disparities. Furthermore, it is the nonunionized employees who are driving up the costs of the institution, so it is unfair to blame unionization for the financial failures of our public and private institutions.

The University as Hedge Fund

Perhaps the main way that universities are now acting like banks is that they have shifted their priorities toward investments and away from education and research. To understand this process, we can look at some of UC's actions during the great California budget fiasco. It turns out that after UC had its state funding cut by $812 million, the university borrowed $200 million and then lent that money to the state. When Yudof was asked how UC could make this type of deal at a time when it was eliminating classes and reducing the pay of most of its employees, he responded that when the university lends money to the state, it makes a profit; in contrast, if that money is spent on continuing costs, like the salaries of teachers, the money disappears.[15] According to this logic, UC should get out of the education business and concentrate on purely profit-centered schemes.

In fact, universities and colleges across the nation have been moving in this direction of cutting instructional activities, while they move funds to the supposedly money-generating sectors. In the case of the UC system, the president of the UC Faculty Association discovered that one reason why the university continues to raise student tuition and fees was that it has promised bond holders it could use student money as collateral for its construction bonds.[16] Furthermore, this system of directing money away from instruction and to construction highlights a general process: universities try to please bond rating companies by showing off diverse revenue streams and large pools of highly liquid assets. Why do universities care so much about bond raters? Much of what universities now do requires borrowing money, and the best way of driving down the costs of borrowing is to get a high bond rating, which enables universities to get a low interest rate.

Universities are therefore doing a lot to impress bond raters, and the main way they do so is to show that they are able to reduce labor costs and diversify revenue streams. In fact, I have found that the best way to understand the priorities of a university is to read its bond ratings. For instance, in 2010, at the same time the UC system was claiming a dire financial emergency, Moody's gave it a high rating for its financial health.[17] In contrast to the university's claims to its faculty, staff, and students, Moody's concluded that the university had maintained a "sizable balance sheet that remains highly liquid, with $3.5 billion of unrestricted financial resources ($5.9 billion excluding post-retirement health liabilities) and active treasury management monitoring a short-term investment pool exceeding $10 billion."[18] In other words, while the university administration was arguing that it had limited access to unrestricted funds, it is clear that it had close to $16 billion to use as it chose.

The claim that an institution does not have any reserves or that its money is all restricted is made by many university presidents. In fact, Howard Bunsis, a professor of accounting at Eastern Michigan University, has used bond rating reports and the audited financial statements of several universities to show how these schools have misrepresented their true financial health in order to impose furloughs, layoffs, wage freezes, and tuition increases. In the case of Rutgers University, he discovered that even though administrators declared in 2010 that a fiscal emergency meant that no staff or faculty would get promised salary increases, the university had access to millions of dollars of unrestricted funds.[19] Bunsis and Gwendolyn Bradley, of the American Association of University Professors, have also found the same pattern at many other universities. In an article in *Inside Higher Ed*, Bunsis and Bradley reveal that several public universities that have imposed furloughs did not have to resort to this cost-cutting measure: "For example, at the University of Northern Iowa, total revenues increased from $269,722,087 in 2009 to $292,646,325 in 2010, despite a decline in the state appropriation, while total expenses declined due to furloughs. As a result, university revenues exceeded expenses by $25.9 million—much more than the $14 million excess in the year previous. At the University of New Mexico, where state appropriations dropped by 10 percent or $30 million in 2010, the decline was more than overcome by increase in tuition and other revenue; the year's revenue exceeded expenses by $100 million."[20] In other words, as public universities have seen their state funding reduced, they have been able to increase their total revenue by increasing tuition and finding other sources of funding. But they never want to reveal this fact, so one has to look at their bond ratings to get a full disclosure of their financial status.

Bunsis and Bradley also point out that most university funds are restricted only by the priorities of the administration: "Administrators tend to speak as though restricted or designated funds are unavailable to them when it comes to balancing the budget—but this is often simply not true. The restrictions and designations represent decisions and priorities, many of which are grievously misplaced. What else can you call it when presidents, coaches, and top administrators earn hundreds of thousands of dollars a year or more but institutions 'can't afford' to give raises to the adjunct faculty who teach the bulk of undergraduate courses while earning low per-course wages? When institutions sink millions into new buildings while class sizes rise?"[21] According to this analysis, university administrators use the false claim of restricted funds in order to argue that they have no choice but to raise tuition and cut instructional expenses when states reduce their budgets.

Another important point made by Bunsis and Bradley's article is that administrators are using claims of a fiscal emergency to push faculty out of the way and undermine shared governance: "Curricular decisions are primarily the responsibility of the faculty, who have the expertise necessary to plan and deliver educational offerings. Absent true financial exigency, program discontinuances should be determined by educational factors, considered by the faculty as a whole or an appropriate committee thereof." What many universities have done is declare a fiscal emergency and use the supposed crisis to impose their agendas and circumvent shared governance and the input of faculty members. Creative accounting is thus a key to how universities in "crisis" are able to increase their revenues as they claim poverty.

One way that universities hide unrestricted funds is by using healthcare and retirement liabilities to offset their assets. For example, in 2010 UC declared a retiree healthcare liability of $2.4 billion, but in reality it paid only $300 million that year into the healthcare system for retirees. This is all perfectly legal—it is even required by accounting rules—but it functions to move large sums of money from unrestricted to restricted funds. Thus, universities can argue that they have no money when they are calling for tuition increases and faculty salaries cuts, but when they simultaneously try to borrow more money, they can claim that they really do have access to large sums of money that they can use for any purpose.[22]

This system of accounting also helps to explain why universities are always undertaking expensive construction projects, even as they reduce instructional spending and increase tuition. By borrowing huge sums of money, universities are able to increase their credit and gain access to more money. Thus, in Moody's bond rating of the UC system, we find the following statement: "Significant capital needs likely to result in rising borrowing levels; debt outstanding has grown from $8.3 billion in

FY2006 to over $13.2 billion in FY2009 and including new borrowings since the end of the fiscal year, a 56% increase."[23] One might think that this high level of debt would hurt the university's bond rating, but in fact Moody's suggests that the university take on more debt: "With expendable financial resources covering pro-forma debt by 0.8 times (resources as of end of FY2009 and debt as of current issue), and debt service consuming 4.1% of operating expenses, we believe the University retains additional debt capacity at the current rating level." Like Third World countries relying on huge loans from the World Bank, universities are not only pushed to take on more debt, but they are also motivated by the bond raters to stop relying on state funding and reduce their exposure to organized labor. Thus, Moody's warns UC about "high susceptibility to regulatory and government pay or changes, coupled with unique stresses on California healthcare, including unionized labor." In this seemingly neutral economic assessment, we find a bias against state regulation, unions, healthcare, and state funding. In other words, the bond raters impose a neoliberal agenda on universities by pushing them to borrow more money as they tell them to privatize their operations and avoid union contracts and state funding.

Moody's also helped to dictate UC's policies by slipping into its analysis the idea that the university should increase the number of students coming from outside of the state: "In-state demand is so strong that UC does little recruiting of freshman from out-of-state. Moody's views this as an untapped strategic asset because UC could easily increase its student demand further if it followed national recruiting practices similar to most peer universities." Not only does Moody's think that the university should accept more out-of-state students, but this noneducational rating agency suggests that the university should spend more money marketing and recruiting students from outside of California.

It is also interesting to note that although the bond raters indicate that UC needs to wean itself off of the unstable support for instruction from the state, they believe the university will continue to profit from the money it gets from the federal government to do research: "The UC system collectively represents a vital part of the nation's research infrastructure, as evidenced by its status as the largest university recipient of federal R&D spending in the country. Total grants and contract revenue in FY2009 exceeded $4.5 billion, with research expenditures exceeding $3.7 billion. Grant and contract revenue has grown consistently in recent years, and given the University's prominent research position we expect it to benefit from a spike in federal research funding provided by the federal stimulus bill."[24] According to this analysis, research grants brought in an $800 million profit in 2009, and this amount may increase due to the federal stimulus package. Hidden in this analysis is the idea that state-funded instruction is unstable, but federally funded grants are a growth market. But as we will see in the next chapter, in reality it is not clear if federal grants make or lose money, and they are an even less stable source of funding than state support.

Moody's not only tells universities, in subtle and not-so-subtle ways, how to spend money, but its raters also push a risky mode of investment: "The long-term targets for the endowment pool would bring alternative assets (including hedge funds, real estate and private equity) to 35% of the total, with domestic and international equity accounting for another 45% of total assets."[25] Even though the move to increase investments in hedge funds, real estate, and private equity could result in a major reduction of endowment wealth, Moody's often shows a preference for this type of investment strategy.

What I am pointing out here is that many public and private research universities may be basing their most important decisions on the opinions of noneducational bond raters. Like corporations, universities are pressured to pursue money-making activities, which means that nonprofit organizations start focusing on profit-generating activities. Furthermore, these profits cannot be spent on things like instruction, because instruction simply uses up money and does not show a future return. Construction projects are all about the future, however, and they are the central reasons for new bonds and new borrowing. In turn, the more money that is generated by the profit-making sectors like housing, parking, and medical services, the more money can be redirected toward compensation for the employees who are alredy earning the highest pay.

The secret history of American research universities that I have been uncovering here is that the more these institutions grow and diversify their activities, the more they are taken over by an administrative class that sees them not as educational institutions but as investment banks and hedge funds. As we shall see in the next chapter, one of the key driving forces behind this financialization of higher education is the role played by research. It turns out that not only does research often have very little connection to instructional quality, but the emphasis on research can actually undermine the ability to teach undergraduates in an effective manner as it drives up the costs of tuition.

7

The High Cost of Research

American research universities have played an essential role in the world economy and the development of many important new technologies and medical innovations. In fact, without the research done at these institutions, we probably would not have the Internet, cellphones, most vaccines, and many other inventions that make our lives easier and more sustainable. However, this investment in research comes at a large cost, and one of the main reasons why tuition goes up and instructional quality goes down in higher education is that externally funded research changes the priorities at these institutions. Moreover, the way that research is supported serves to undermine one of the core values of modern science: the unbiased pursuit of truth through open inquiry.[1] To make this argument, I will explore how sponsored research often hurts teaching and how universities are losing their commitment to science, while they pursue expensive side projects.

Research versus Teaching

It is a hot, sunny summer day on a UC campus, and I am surrounded by science faculty who are taking a break from a meeting. One young professor says to another, "Yeah, I have to do three next year, but they promised me only one the following year." The rest of the conversation that I am overhearing lets me translate this cryptic phrase into: "I have to teach three courses next year, but the chair of my department promised me that

I have to teach only one course the following year." This sentence alone tells us much about the problematic relationship between research and instruction at American research universities. First of all, this professor is teaching in a quarter system and he has the summer quarter off, so he is complaining about teaching one course during each session in the next year. Moreover, the course is seen as a burden rather than as an integral part of his job. Second, he has made a private deal with the head of his department so that he will teach only one course the following year. In other words, during a two-year period, he will teach only four classes. During the same time period, a full-time untenured lecturer in his program, making a third of his salary, will be teaching eighteen courses. Also, this professor's lab will be filled with low-wage graduate students and postdoctorates who might have to go on food stamps to be able to afford living in this expensive city. Not only does this system undermine any sense of justice and equality in higher education, but it shows how perverse incentives shape the attitudes of research faculty.

As many other people have argued, universities undermine education and teaching by basing tenure, promotion, and merit increases for some professors on research.[2] To move up in this system, therefore, one needs to produce a book or important article, get an outside research grant, or patent a new technology. A new professor quickly learns that it is possible to advance even if you can put very little effort into your teaching and get horrible student evaluations. In other words, some professors at research universities are socialized to believe that they will be rewarded only for doing research and bringing money and prestige to the university from the outside world. In turn, many universities think that the only way they can survive the constant reductions in state funding for higher education is to shift more of their focus to research and revenue-generating activities. However, not only does this process threaten to turn universities into corporations, but it also changes every aspect of an educational institution.[3]

Good books have been written on the relationship between research and teaching, but none of them have devoted much attention to how undergraduate education is affected by this change in priorities.[4] As I will show, not only do professors often have no incentive to become good teachers, but they also have little incentive to care about the university as a shared community.[5] And because there is no incentive for high-paid research professors to teach in an effective manner, forcing them into the undergraduate classroom helps to drive up costs and drive down the quality of instruction.

It is important to stress that we still need to support research and research universities because they play a central role in the development of knowledge, technology, and creativity throughout the world. Thus, unlike Andrew Hacker and Claudia Dreifus in *Higher Education?*, I will not be arguing that we should simply spin research off from universities. Instead, I believe that we need to defend research as the scientific and creative investigation of truth, but we also need to make sure that the research mission does not undermine instruction and force tuition to go up. Moreover, we have to guard against the corrupting nature of some sponsored research. After all, the main reason why so many corporations and governmental entities go to universities to develop and test their products and discoveries is that universities are supposed to provide an unbiased scientific perspective. Yet the more universities rely on outside forces for funding, the more susceptible those universities are to pressures to slant their research and conclusionss according to the desires and needs of the external funding sources. Just as large campaign donations corrupt democracy, big external grants threaten to undermine the scientific basis of university research.

Even worse than its hindering of the search for truth, research can block the effective communication of truth and knowledge in the classroom. One of the most visible signs of the negative influence of research is putting professors who have not mastered the English language in the classroom. This all-too-common practice makes a mockery of education and sends the clear message to undergraduates that the university does not think their education matters. I am often asked why universities make people who are obviously not capable of being good teachers teach, and my response is twofold: universities believe in the idea that research and teaching are a unified activity, and universities receive a lot of state funding and tuition dollars based on the notion that it is not possible to separate research from teaching.[6] After all, the reason why students go to a research university is so they can be taught by great researchers—and even though many of these researchers never do teach, they are still on campus and bring the aura and prestige of research to the university.

It is also important to stress that most states base their per student contribution to their public research universities on the idea that research professors will be teaching all of the classes. Moreover, states use a formula called the research and instructional budget, and there is no agreed-on way of dividing the different parts of a professor's job. Thus, everyone accepts the fiction that research and teaching go hand in hand.[7] States and students pay the salaries of research professors who do little, if any, teaching; and in order to staff the classes, universities have to rely on inexpensive graduate students and untenured faculty to replace the professors. What often happens is that a professor gets an external grant that includes money to buy the professor out of his or her teaching duties, so the university uses this money to hire someone else to take the professor's place in the classroom. Thus, the state ends up paying for people to teach, but they end up doing a different job. However, my argument here is not that we should force research professors to teach; rather, we need to make the funding system clear so parents, students, and legislators can know what they are really supporting.

Taken for Granted

The complicated grant system for researchers is rarely understood or examined, and no one seems to know if external research grants actually bring universities a profit or end up costing more money than they bring in.[8] One reason why it is impossible to determine the overall profit margin for grants is that most grants are tied to what is called "indirect costs." For example, if a professor applies to the federal government for a $100,000 grant to develop laser technology for eye surgery, the grant is normally for $150,000: $100,000 for direct costs (equipment, salaries, and utilities), and $50,000 for indirect costs (central administration, staff, maintenance, buildings, and libraries). These indirect costs are determined by a general, abstract formula that says something like for every grant, 10 percent should go to the institution's central administration, 15 percent to staffing, 5 percent to energy costs, 10 percent to utilities, and 1 percent to libraries.[9] The idea behind indirect costs, then, is that every research project relies on there being staff, central administration, buildings, labs, and electricity, and so forth, and thus every grant should pay into a common fund.

But there is no way of knowing if a particular grant is paying too much or too little into the shared costs. After all, it may take a lot of staff and legal experts to oversee a study of pharmaceutical drugs, but the same costs do not apply to a grant that looks at the wing speed of wasps. Likewise, a lab that examines the movement of subatomic particles costs a lot of money, but a researcher studying the movement of stocks in relation to inflation may require very little lab equipment—yet the university will charge both external grants the same percentage for lab and utility costs.

Since no one knows if grants end up earning or costing money, professors and administrators often fight over the value of relying on external funds at research universities. Many professors in the humanities believe that universities favor the sciences because these fields bring in so much grant money, but it is unclear whether high-paid science professors with expensive labs bring in any real profit. In fact, as I showed in chapter 2, undergraduate courses in the humanities turn a large profit because they use relatively cheap labor to teach a large number of students, and they do not use expensive lab equipment. According to a strictly cost-benefit analysis, humanities departments should be receiving increased funding so they can continue to teach more students at a reduced cost, but this is not what happens at research universities.[10] Instead, public university administrators argue that because the people teaching courses in the humanities are paid out of state funds and student tuition and do not bring in many research grants, they cannot be profitable. These administrators see science professors, who do bring in external grants, as profit-making even though they too are paid out of state funds and tuition and they may cost the university money and draw resources away from instruction.

One possible result of the growing reliance on research grants at research universities is that the sciences are actually losing money and relying on relatively inexpensive classes in the humanities to make up for their losses. Yet another possibility is that research grants actually make profits, and these profits are being used to fuel increases in compensation for star professors and administrators. According to the latter theory, the funds brought in through the indirect costs of external grants generate a huge pot of money that can be allocated to any purpose. Moreover, no one can quite determine what happens to the money that states and students pay for research professors who are also paid out of external grants.

For example, when a professor gets a grant that allows him to buy himself out of his teaching responsibilities, and the professor is then replaced by a part-time teacher who makes a much lower salary, what happens to the money from the state or the tuition dollars that were supposed to go toward the professor's salary? No one seems able to answer this question.

I believe it is highly likely that some grants lose money and some grants make money, and there is no way to know if a particular project is profitable or not. There is also no way of knowing if universities lose or gain money overall from research.[11] However, we do know that money from student tuition and state funding that is earmarked for instruction ends up being used for research, although it is rare for any money that is made through research to end up funding teaching. In other words, funds flow in only one direction, and the result is that instructional dollars are reduced as research budgets are increased.[12] And because the push for more research can cause an increase the number and cost of bureaucrats to administer grants, once again the result is fewer teachers, more administrators, and less money to spend on instruction.

This conflict between research and instruction is compounded by the fact that many universities create a strict division between the money that can be spent on instruction and the money that can be used for other purposes. For instance, during the University of California's supposed budget crisis of 2009, Mark Yudof declared that fees would have to be raised and courses eliminated because the state had reduced the university's budget by $800 million. When Yudof was asked why he could not just use money from other sources, like research profits, to make up for the state reductions, he replied that the money generated by research grants is legally restricted and cannot be used to fund teaching positions.[13] By clinging to the fiction that only tuition and state dollars can pay for instructional costs, Yudof was really saying that state and student dollars can fund research, but research does not have to return the favor. He also reiterated the idea that profit-making sectors should be able to keep their money, while non-profit-oriented units, like undergraduate instruction, would have to make sacrifices. When the university decided to impose a salary reduction (called a furlough) on all of its employees, people funded out of external grants were excluded from the program; to make up for that loss of savings, the instructional budget had to be cut even further.[14]

How Research Changes Teaching

Not only does the push for more research drain instructional budgets, but it also changes the content and the quality of undergraduate education. Most research universities force research professors to do some teaching, so the professors' research agendas show up in the classroom. In other words, if a psychology department receives a lot of money from pharmaceutical companies to test the quality of particular psychiatric drugs, the department will hire more professors who believe that chemistry determines our mental states, and they will teach students theories that stress biological over sociological causes of behavior. Also, many research grants come with secrecy agreements that prevent professors from publishing or even discussing any negative results they find.[15] Not only do these agreements prevent professors from talking to each other, but they also can determine what a teacher can and cannot say in the classroom.

As many studies of grant-funded research have shown, it is often difficult for someone funded by a particular corporation to make any strong criticism of its products.[16] After all, if your future research and earnings depend on an external company, you have a lot of incentives to please that outside interest group. Companies go to universities to study their products because universities are considered to be objective, neutral, and unbiased, but the more universities rely on funded research, the less objective and neutral they become. Moreover, this loss of objectivity and neutrality has to affect the classroom: research professors are being influenced by external forces, and these professors teach large lecture classes in which students don't have a chance to question the meaning or rightness of the theories being presented. Biased research is presented as being universal truth, and students are then tested on their ability to memorize and repeat the results of this questionable research on standardized, multiple-choice exams. In other words, students are being trained to accept without criticism expert scientific research, while the experts are being paid by companies to sometimes do little more than verify predetermined results.

Research and the Exploitation of Graduate Students

One reason, then, why universities may not want to have more small, inter-active courses is that some professors do not want to have their research and theories challenged in class. However, as explained above, I believe that the main reason why research universities prefer large classes is to provide jobs for graduate students. Graduate students also provide rela-tively cheap labor as research assistants in science labs, and the use of these students helps to drive down the cost of doing research. Given that the most expensive aspect of developing new products is the research and design stage, universities offer a relatively cheap way of designing and test-ing new technologies and products for major corporations and govern-mental programs. In this system, state and student funds are used to build expensive labs and pay the salaries of professors and graduate students; companies basically rent the use of these workers and labs at a very low price. The system may help to spur economic growth, but it has the unin-tended consequence of exploiting graduate students and transforming what is taught in the classroom.

Not only are researchers motivated to base the content of their teach-ing on the area of their funded research, but they also soon find out that external grants bring the university prestige and high rankings as well as money. And because the number and value of grants is often used to rank graduate programs, universities have a great incentive to push their faculty into grant-funded research. Moreover, due to the fact that undergraduate and graduate programs are not rated for the quality of their teachers or the learning of their students, faculty and institutions realize that prestige comes only from external recognition. This means that published research becomes key to personal advancement.[17] According to this logic, a profes-sor can make a lot more money if he or she receives grants and publishes research; teaching, in contrast, serves only to soak up the professor's time and prevents pay raises.

Big Research

Jennifer Washburn's "Big Oil Goes to College" helps explain how research can transform a university. Washburn points out that in 2010, only 6 percent of university research was funded by outside corporations; however, nearly 25 percent of the total research done at research universities involved public-private partnerships.[18] In other words, research is now being funded by a combination of sources, and these partnerships can produce multiple conflicts of interest. In her extensive analysis of ten different public-private partnerships at research universities, Washburn found that "in a majority of the 10 contracts, the university gave up majority control over the governing body in charge of the university-industry research alliance, and in four cases actually ceded full control to the participating corporations."[19] Thus, one of the corrupting effects of this type of research arrangement is that universities give up their control of institutional decisions, which can result in outside corporations deciding which faculty members get funding, and what university rules apply to different research projects.

A related issue highlighted by Washburn is the control over when and how research is published and discussed: "While the contracts preserve the university's right to publish, several allow for long publication delays, in one case as long as seven months, and in another as long as one year."[20] This kind of arrangement goes against the central notion that universities are supposed to freely pursue truth, and their findings should be presented to the public in a free and open manner. Instead, what often happens in funded research is that the funder can control who has access to new knowledge and research. In fact, Washburn found that due to secrecy agreements, public-private partnerships at research universities often block the peer review process that is so essential to the scientific method. Due to the restrictions placed on funded research, faculty are often told that they can not discuss their research with other researchers, and the discoveries made in this type of arrangement often do not result in any added revenue for universities because the corporations can control the intellectual property rights.

Washburn stresses that although many universities spend a great deal of money chasing external grants, most of them end up losing money or failing to gain income through their external funding: "Only roughly two dozen U.S. universities generate sizable income from all this heightened commercial activity due to a few blockbuster inventions that generate revenue."[21] And she notes that the integrity of universities' research and shared governance is compromised: "A large body of analytical and empirical research finds that industry-sponsored research is far more likely to favor the corporate sponsor's products and/or commercial interests compared to government- or non-profit-funded research."[22] Washburn discusses several instances where research has proven to be compromised:

> One meta-analysis, combining a wide array of studies, found that pharmaceutical industry-funded research was four times more likely to reflect favorably on a drug, compared with research not funded by industry. Another study found that scientific review articles on the effects of secondhand smoke exposure written by researchers with industry ties were 88 times more likely to find no harm, compared with articles penned by researchers with no industry ties. In published studies comparing different brands of cholesterol drugs head-to-head, the drug that comes out looking better is 20 times more likely to have been manufactured by the company funding the study. In the field of nutrition, one detailed analysis of 206 studies of milk, fruit juice, and soft drinks found that, when a company sponsored studies of its own or a competitor's products, the results were four to eight times more likely to be favorable to the company's financial interests than studies funded independently.[23]

These studies show why the turn to externally funded research is such a dangerous proposition for research universities, undermining both pure research and the fundamental values guiding these institutions.

Research outside the Sciences

It is clear how this research paradigm affects the sciences, but its impact on the humanities is less clear. After all, who really cares if a comparative literature professor publishes another book on Dante? Furthermore, very few humanities scholars receive external grants or engage in other types of revenue-generating activities.[24] Yet universities still privilege the research paradigm in the humanities because research is the key to prestige and external reputation. Thus, tenure and promotion in the humanities are based on research, so teaching is once again short-changed. To make matters worse, because humanities scholars do not bring in a lot of research money, their research activities must be paid for out of instructional funds.

One justification that I have heard for why fields like English and philosophy stress research over teaching is that famous researchers attract the best graduate students—that is, the ones with the highest test scores. The idea here is that if a university has a professor who has written a well-respected book on Dante, that professor will attract all of the good graduate students who are also interested in Dante. Moreover, due to the professor's fame, other schools will give his or her department a high ranking. Prestige is based only on external recognition, so faculty are trained to see people outside of their own institution as the key audience for their work.[25] This incentive system not only means that professors will spend less time concentrating on teaching and committee work, but also that they will always be on the market for a better outside job offer. Once again, this process inflates salaries as it undermines instruction.

The dominance of research in the humanities and the social sciences may also be partly due to the fact that in the fight for internal prestige, nonscience subjects have to take on the structure and form of scientific research. In other words, nonscientists can gain credibility only if they present their research in a scientific manner. And because it is easier to count books and articles to assess a candidate for tenure and promotion than it is to quantify the quality of that person's teaching, once again research wins out over instruction. Some great researchers are also great teachers who bring their cutting-edge research into the classroom, but the incentive system pushes many professors to privilege research over teaching. The system is so one-sided that I have heard faculty members disparage other professors because they have won teaching awards. According to the logic of research universities, if students think you are a great teacher, you must be spending too much time on instruction and not enough time on research.

As I will argue in the final chapters of this book, we must change this system by creating professorial positions for researchers and other positions for teachers. Furthermore, we need to base the ranking and reputation of schools and departments on the quality of their teachers. By changing incentive systems, we can motivate institutions to prioritize undergraduate instruction. However, as I will show in the next chapter, these reforms may be blocked by the way universities are turning to technology to make teaching more efficient and less costly. It turns out that not only do new technologies often drive up the cost of instruction, but they also contribute to the degradation of instructional quality.

8

Technology to the Rescue?

I am sitting on an Amtrak train trying to finish reading a novel, but I cannot concentrate because I am surrounded by people speaking—no, yelling—into their cellphones. Right behind me is a young college student who has two papers due the next day, one in history and one in English. I know this because she has called at least five different people to talk about how much work she has to do and how she will never finish it in time. I want to turn around and suggest to her that if she just got off the phone, she could start her work, but I do not want to intrude in her personal space.

The next day as I am walking out of class, I see hundreds of students leave a lecture class, and almost all of them immediately take out their cellphones or their iPods. They look like some alien army that needs to be hooked into a secret energy source. When I later ask my students why so many students get on their cellphones right after class, they tell me that they want to reconnect with friends or just "check in." I then ask them what they think students did after class back in the old days—say ten years ago—when everyone did not have portable phones. Students look very confused when I pose this question, as if I was asking them how people would walk around without gravity. One student once sheepishly raised his hand and said that back in the day, everyone must have run to pay phones. This response made me laugh, and everyone else laughed nervously, until another student raised her hand and said, "People used to smoke after class, so at least now, we are, like, a lot healthier." This response threw me off because I had never thought about this possibility, but still I was not satisfied. I asked them again, "What do you think people could do after a class instead of texting a friend or listening to music?" After a prolonged silence, a student replied, "You want us to say that the students talked about the class, don't you?" I responded that I was hoping that someone might mention that possibility, but that there are other things people could do, like reflect on their own lives or just look at nature. This final comment prompted a series of confused looks; students just don't seem to understand why someone would simply want to think or look.

Some of my students tell me that they feel they are addicted to technologies, and many students admit that between each class, they check their Facebook pages to see if they have received any new postings. Students report how freaked out they were when they lost their cellphones, or explain that their essay is late because their printer would not work. It appears that we are really entering into a new digital age, and college students today do have a very different ways of working and communicating. The question, then, is how universities should adapt to these changes, and how new technologies can make education more effective.

The "Smart" Classroom

Many universities have responded to these technological innovations by wiring their campuses and making the Web free and accessible from all locations. In fact, the push for "smart" classrooms has cost schools a tremendous amount of money, and rarely do administrators or faculty ask if this money is well spent or what effects these technologies will have on student learning.[1] In order to examine the question of whether new computer technologies actually promote or prevent education at research universities, I decided to teach all of my courses in networked classrooms. In fact, I helped to design a new high-tech classroom, and although it was never built, this experience taught me a lot about why universities often spend so much and get so little back for their money in this area.

The first striking thing about teaching in a networked classroom, where each student is sitting behind a computer monitor, is that you never know what the students are actually doing. Not only do the computer screens often block their faces, but the Internet gives the students the opportunity to look like they are working while they are really playing games, checking sports scores, e-mailing their friends, or buying new shoes. The only way to know what they are really doing in class is to check the history function on their individual computers, which is something I once did. I was dismayed to discover that many of the students were actually playing games, checking sports scores, e-mailing their friends, and buying new shoes. After this experience, I started telling my students that if they surfed the Web during class, I would be sent a message, and they would fail the course.

I thought this intervention was great, until a student came up to me almost in tears because she felt she could not pass the class due to her inability not to multitask. She told me that the only way she can write or take notes is if she is doing something else at the same time, and if she couldn't listen to music or text her friends during class, she didn't think she would be able to do any work. I really did not know how to counsel this student, but I began to ask students about multitasking, and I found that most of my students are always doing many things at the same time.[2] For instance, when they sit in large lecture classes, they are usually texting their friends, reading the news, or even watching movies. Some students admitted that they go to the library to write a paper and spend several hours, then realize that they have been texting and playing games the whole time. It turns out that laptops are very confusing objects because they combine in one place a workstation and a virtual playground.[3]

I do not want to discount the tremendous possibilities that computers and the Web offer students, but it is disheartening that many of the people promoting new technologies in higher education have never studied how students actually use these tools.[4] To many administrators, new technologies always offer the possibility of doing more for less.[5] For example, universities often offer grants to faculty who can develop ways of using new technologies to make large lecture classes seem small. A recent example of a project that received major funding was the creation of a special type of remote control—"the clicker"—that students can use to participate in large classes. The idea here is that each student is assigned a clicker and a number, and periodically the professor stops the lecture and asks students to respond to a multiple-choice question. After the students answer by pressing the appropriate button on their clicker, the results of the instant test are revealed on the big screen. Not only does this system allow students to participate, but it also helps teachers to keep attendance. However, we must ask, what kind of active learning is really being pursued here?[6]

Another major funding initiative at UCLA was to record and Webcast lectures so students could review them at a later date. This seemed like a good idea at the time, but it turned out that once the lecturers were online, students simply stopped going to class. It appears that when universities think they have found a way of using technology to make classes more effective or efficient, it often backfires on them.[7] For example, some professors have received a lot of money to design a computer system that would allow students to mark each other's papers in a safe and anonymous way. This complicated peer review system was supposed to save the university money by not having to hire graduate students to mark essays, and the grant application also proclaimed that the new technology would help students become better writers by reading and marking other students' papers.[8] However, one of my students told me that some of his friends quickly found a way of gaming the system, and they used special signal words in their papers to tell their friends which papers were theirs and thus should receive a high grade. I also discovered from the same source that students use their cellphones to take pictures of exam questions, send the pictures to their friends who are home with access to computers and books, and get the answers back by phone.

Some people may say that I am being cynical; rather, I am trying to be realistic by looking at the actual practices and attitudes of today's students. After all, from a very young age, their parents and the educational system have rewarded them for grades and not for learning, so it is perfectly logical for them to do anything they can to receive high grades.[9] As so many psychologists have shown, if you train people by giving them only external rewards, they may never develop inner motivation. Some college students are virtually addicted to high grades and new technologies, and when these two things come together, they acquire an awesome power.

To further examine the interaction between learning and technology, I had my students interview other students about how they study and research. Many of my young researchers discovered that virtually every student starts a written assignment by using Google and Wikipedia. I had known that these online tools were very popular, but I had not realized to what extent they dominate students' studying habits. Now, I do not want to say that these sites are not helpful and important, but I do want to question why teachers just pretend that they do not exist. In fact, I have found that virtually the only time faculty mention Wikipedia is to tell students not to use it, which is like telling students not to have sex or drink beer. What we should be telling students is how to use these tools in a responsible fashion. Of course, many professors spend little time thinking about how their students actually study or do research, and the focus of many university courses is on distributing information and testing students' absorption of it, instead of developing their critical thinking, speaking, and writing skills.

PowerPoint Corrupts Absolutely

Although professors often resist changing their teaching styles and incorporating new technologies into their classes, one technology that has become quite popular in large lecture classes is PowerPoint. This new mode of computer-mediated knowledge distribution may be more legible than the professor's handwriting on a blackboard, but it does not necessarily help students learn.[10] Furthermore, the way information is presented in PowerPoint slides often does a disservice to students' writing and thinking. For example, many professors simply list points in an outline fashion, and this type of writing can disconnect ideas and usually ignores the important need for transitions and logical connections. In fact, my students reported in their research on how other students use technology to learn and study that many classmates claim they spend much of their time in class feverishly copying what the professor puts on PowerPoint slides, and when they later study for tests, they sometimes have no idea what their notes mean. Students also tell me that they have never been taught how to study or take notes in a large class, so they try to copy everything down. Luckily for some overwhelmed students, professors now put their PowerPoint slides online, but this means that some students just use the online resources and don't go to class, so they miss any explanations that the teacher gives there.

Not only do new technologies often make classroom attendance optional, but they also can function to make students happy even while the quality of their education goes down. For instance, students may be content in large lecture classes because with their laptops, they can do whatever they want. I can imagine some people responding to this statement by insisting that the university must surely want students to learn, but I would reply that many of the people now running universities have no background in education and see things strictly in terms of efficiency.

As an example, once when I was teaching in my networked classroom, a staff person interrupted the class to tell me that I was using the lab too much and that I should not schedule all of my classes in the room. I responded that the lab was my only classroom, and unlike other teachers, who used the room only occasionally, my entire course was based on computer-mediated education. I was then told that I could use the room, but my use of software licenses would be limited so that only two students could use the software at the same time.

Countless other faculty have had bad experiences when they try to use new technologies.[11] For instance, many teachers have complained that the staff in computer labs do not know how to use some of the basic programs, a problem I experienced over and over again.[12] In each class that I taught, I was assigned a student helper, who was being paid to make the class run smoothly. Unfortunately, these students had no knowledge of the basic Web courseware program that all faculty were supposed to use, and in virtually every class, what ended up happening was that the student helper would sit next to me in front of the class and spend the whole time surfing the Web or playing video games. I always wondered what kind of message this obvious lack of interest conveyed to the other students in the class. When I told the staff supervisor about this problem, she told me that her job was to hire the students, not to train them.[13]

The High Cost of New Technology

Ultimately, the debate over how to use technology to make university classes more effective and efficient is flawed because it does not look at all of the indirect and direct ways that new technologies draw money away from the instructional mission. In most cases, to set up a computer classroom or computerized lab, one needs to pay for staff, administrators, electricity, equipment, software licenses, and endless training sessions. Moreover, adopting new technologies often results in hiring staff with no direct experience or background in education, and they make decisions that do not take into consideration important instructional concerns.

In his article "The Costs and Costing of Online Learning," Greville Rumble looks at the actual costs of using online courses at research universities. His main finding is that previous research on this topic failed to take into account all the related expenses: "One of the problems with many of the studies now available is that they report the broad results, not the detail. It is therefore difficult to know what has been included and what excluded, and so whether the costings undertaken are comprehensive. Experience suggests, however, that all figures need to be treated with care. What does seem clear is that the costs of developing a course are being pushed up— and significantly so whenever media are used in a sophisticated way. If so, and if cost efficiency is an important consideration, then savings may need to be looked for in delivery."[14] Rumble here argues that one of the main cost drivers in online courses is the development of the class material. In fact, his research shows that if universities want to produce a high-quality educational experience, they have to spend a great deal of money: "The high costs of developing internet courses are confirmed by Saba, who suggests that commercial software companies developing courses for online instruction or publishers are spending at least $500,000 to fully develop a multimedia course."[15] It is important to note that when universities present the cost of new online programs, they usually do not account for the initial costs of course development.

Rumble also believes that although these new programs are often used to save labor costs and faculty time, the opposite often happens:

A high proportion of the costs of developing materials is labor costs. All the research shows that it takes more academic time to develop media that will occupy a student for one hour, than it takes to develop a one-hour lecture—although how much more time is difficult to quantify. Sparkes reckoned that it took from 2 to 10 hours to prepare a lecture, from 1 to 10 hours to prepare a small group session, and from 3 to 10 hours to prepare a video-tape lecture; however, it took at least 50 to 100 academic hours to prepare a teaching text, 100 hours to prepare a television broadcast, 200 hours to develop computer-aided learning, and 300 hours to develop interactive materials—to which in all cases one needed to add the time of technical support staff.[16]

There are thus a lot of hidden costs involved in developing online courses, and these expenses rarely show up in presentations on the cost-effectiveness of computer-mediated education.

Universities also sometimes underestimate the expenses related to delivering online courses: "In general none of the studies undertaken to date adequately factor in the costs of overheads. Although, the costs of putting in equipment directly associated with the projects (e.g., servers) are usually taken into account, as are the costs of software licenses, college operating budgets do not usually reflect the full costs of maintaining networked services."[17] It turns out that it is very hard to calculate the total cost of software licenses, network maintenance, and equipment for online programs, so universities simply make a guess and present it as a fact.

And universities have a hard time predicting the number of staff and administrators they will need for a new online program: "Much depends on the context—the time spent agreeing that a group of enthusiasts can develop a project will be very different to that required to change an institution's direction. Indeed, developing an IT [information technology] strategy is likely to be expensive."[18] One thing that we can be sure of is that the use of online courses drives up the cost of administration and staff while further squeezing instructional budgets.

Instructional Costs

We are left with the question of why so many schools see online instruction as the solution for increased costs and rising tuition. One place to look for an answer is the federal government, which has promoted the idea of digital education as an inevitable transformation for higher education. For instance, *Preparing for the Revolution: Information Technology and the Future of the Research University*, a report by the National Research Council, argues that American research universities need to adapt to new technologies, or they will be left behind:

Universities will have to function in a highly digital environment along with other organizations as almost every academic function will be affected, and sometimes displaced, by modern technology. The ways that universities manage their resources, relate to clients and providers, and conduct their affairs will have to be consistent not only with the nature of their own enterprise but also with the reality of "e-everything." As competitors appear, and in many cases provide more effective and less costly alternatives, universities will be forced to embrace new techniques themselves or outsource some of their functions.[19]

Central to this analysis of the role of technology in research universities is the argument that nontraditional, computer-based institutions of higher education will force traditional universities to change. Coupled with this call for research universities to become more efficient and competitive, we find an emphasis on having these traditional institutions provide research and experimentation addressing the proper role of new technologies in higher education.

The potential conflict in this national agenda is that research universities are asked to simultaneously embrace the critical analysis of new technology and to use online courses to reduce costs. In fact, the authors of the report return to a traditional understanding of the modern research university in order to call for a deployment of nontraditional technologies and educational methods: "Learning and scholarship do require some independence from society. The research university in particular provides a relatively cloistered environment in which people can deeply investigate fundamental problems in the natural sciences, social sciences, and humanities, and can learn the art of analyzing difficult problems. But the rapid and substantial changes in store for the university—not only those related to information technology—require that academics work with the institution's many stakeholders to learn of their evolving needs, expectations, and perceptions of higher education."[20] Thus universities are given the task of researching the effectiveness of new educational technologies because these schools are supposed to conduct unbiased research and not be swayed by purely economic considerations; however, the driving force behind this new educational movement is often the desire to cut costs and educate students in a more efficient manner.

This debate over the roles of traditional universities and online education is rendered even more problematic by the way that the National

Research Council's report tends to affirm a false and misleading conception of higher education in a globalized world: "We can now use powerful computers and networks to deliver educational services to anyone—any place, any time. Technology can create an open learning environment in which the student, no longer compelled to travel to a particular location in order to participate in a pedagogical process involving tightly integrated studies based mostly on lectures or seminars by local experts, is evolving into an active and demanding consumer of educational services."[21] This globalizing rhetoric of "anyone—any place, any time" ignores the very real digital divides in our world, and governments and universities often invoke these claims of global access to higher education in order to hide important disparities in access and quality. The report combines the rhetoric of globalization with a contradictory discourse of competition. Thus, research universities are celebrated because they are removed from normal social concerns, but they are also criticized because they have not fully embraced the new technologies.

At the heart of this contradictory representation of research universities is an unacknowledged debate over what values should determine the mission of our institutions of higher education. The report's authors want to affirm the globalizing rhetoric of universal access to education, but they also desire to place research universities in a privileged position. Our universities are therefore supposed to be both egalitarian and hierarchical, above society yet central to the new social order.

These contradictions often work to conceal the growing corporatization of higher education behind a rhetoric of student-centered education and computer-mediated information sharing. For example, the report calls for a radical restructuring of the teacher-student relationship: "We envision a future, enabled by information technology and driven by learner demand, in which two of the major (and taken-for-granted) ways of organizing undergraduate learning will recede in importance: the 55-minute classroom lecture and the common reading list. That digital future will challenge faculty to design technology-based experiences based primarily on interactive, collaborative learning. Although these new approaches will be quite different from traditional ones, they may be far more effective, particularly when provided through a media-rich environment."[22] We can read this call to use technology to make undergraduate education more

collaborative and learner-centered as a positive move to update traditional methods of instruction; however, behind this educational claim, we
find a call to downsize the expertise of faculty:

> Students may be more involved in the creation of learning envi-
> ronments, working shoulder to shoulder with the faculty just as
> they do when serving as research assistants. In that context, stu-
> dent and professor alike are apt to be experts, though in differ-
> ent domains. . . . The faculty member of the twenty-first century
> university could thus become more of a consultant or coach than
> a teacher, less concerned with transmitting intellectual content
> directly than with inspiring, motivating, and managing an active
> learning process.[23]

By turning professors into coaches and facilitators, this model of education unintentionally contributes to the elimination of professors and
tenure. After all, who needs to hire professors with doctorates if the main
role of professors is now to simply help students manage their own learning experiences? Following the logic of the downsizing of journalism, the
music industry, and other traditional fields, the report maps out a plan to
eliminate professors, tenure, and expertise.

The model in the report is actually a plan to promote the end of
research universities and a move to online universities, like the University
of Phoenix. After all, as this report highlights, public research universities have to compete with new modes of education and technology that
are driven by cost-saving and consumer-oriented priorities. According to
the report's authors, the only thing that seems to help maintain the value
and purpose of research universities for many students and parents is the
prestige of particular degrees and the chance to study with expert faculty
members.[24] Yet we must ask what happens in a system where all expertise is shared, and the teacher becomes a coach rather than an important
source of valued information.

UC Goes Digital

Although the research discussed above should make it clear that a turn
to online courses by research universities may not only increase costs but

may also spell the end of expertise and professors, many universities are still pursuing digital education as a solution to budgetary problems. For example, in 2010 the University of California started to develop a new online program to raise funds and streamline undergraduate education. As an initial way of examining this move to online courses, the university put together a Commission on the Future, and in their final report, the commission's members argued that a new digital program would "reduce course impaction, reduce scheduling conflicts, and increase summer session enrollments by enabling students to earn credits without being on campus, thus reducing students' average time to degree."[25] Here, online education is seen as the solution to many of the university's problems; however, hardly any members of the commission had any experience with digital educational programs, and many of them have never been educators. Many UC professors suspect that one of the main goals of this online initiative is to wrest control of the curriculum away from faculty, so that administrators can make decisions without faculty input.

UC administrators have insisted that the faculty will have the final say on what courses are moved online, but the university has already broken several of its promises and appears to be driven by the questionable assumption that online courses are the only thing that can protect the university against state budget cuts. In order to gain approval of the faculty senate for the initiative, the administration promised that it would use outside funds to support the initial pilot program, but after it failed to generate the needed money, it decided to borrow several million dollars from the university reserves to fund the first round of courses. The university also promised that it would first develop a small number of classes and then have these classes examined and tested by the faculty before it would continue with the project; once again, the administration went back on its word and decided that it had to develop a new round of courses quickly, in order to fund the project and pay back the money the university had borrowed from itself.[26]

So far it looks as if the UC system is following the trend of spending more money to lower the quality of education, and the administration appears to be bent on pursuing the online program regardless of the costs. To pitch this program as something more than a cost-saving effort, the university has promoted online instruction as a way of making elite education available to people who are normally excluded from research universities. Here we find the central contradiction discussed in chapter 3, which is that liberal institutions often combine progressive policies with exploitive economic practices. Therefore, although the online program could result in the loss of many faculty positions and the hiring of a permanent underclass of low-wage "facilitators" instead of teachers, the university has claimed that online education is about expanding access to underrepresented minority students.

UC's administration has also been presenting the initiative as financially viable. According to a report in the *Daily Californian*, "Christopher Edley, Jr., dean of the UC Berkeley School of Law and special adviser to the UC President Mark Yudof, said in a presentation that if an online course is offered four times a year and the enrollment for the class is 100 students, the course could generate up to $163,000 for the educating faculty and its department."[27] What is so remarkable about Edley's presentation is that there is no way for him to know how much money a particular course would bring in: he does not know who would teach the course, how much the course would cost to develop, or how much revenue the current courses generate. Following the tradition of promoters of digital education, Edley is simply presenting guesses as if they are facts.

Another interesting element of Edley's presentation is the idea that the faculty in the department offering the online courses would profit from the revenue generated by the courses. At the same time that the UC system is developing this online program, administrators are considering changing the way professors are compensated by allowing them to use outside grants and departmental revenue to augment their base pay. In other words, faculty are being told that they can increase their salaries if they support online courses for their departments. This sounds very much like a bribe.

One problem with this deal is that if faculty turn over control of their courses to the online administrators, they will lose one of their main sources of departmental income, which is the profits derived from inexpensive large lecture classes taught mostly by untenured faculty members. However, most faculty members are unaware of how university budgets work, and they may not realize that accepting the deal would entail the financial destruction of their own programs. For example, the main targets for becoming online courses in the UC system are the lower-division writing, language, math, science, and social science classes. It is true that these required courses have the highest enrollments, but what many faculty members fail to see is that these classes are also the least expensive and the most efficient. Furthermore, these courses are mostly taught by graduate students and untenured lecturers; tenured professors have very little connection to these classes and might not care if they are outsourced or put online. Yet the salaries of the professors are in part paid out of the income generated by these high-demand, inexpensive courses. One has to wonder what will happen when the main sources of enrollments for a department are moved online and these classes become shared between campuses. Not only might the professors lose control of their curricula, but they may lose most of their funding.

Of course, if the university really wanted to save money, it would move its expensive graduate and professional school courses online, but this option is not being discussed because the faculty and the administration know that you cannot provide high-quality education in large online courses. The only reason, then, why the faculty and the administration will accept the move to digital education for lower-division undergraduate courses is that they do not want to defend the importance of these core classes. As we have seen throughout this book, all of the incentives of research universities privilege research over instruction and graduate education over undergraduate education. As a result, professors and administrators may inadvertently commit institutional suicide by killing off their cash cows and neglecting the core mission of their institutions.

Online For-Profit Education

As David Noble has shown, universities are often motivated to get involved in online education because corporations convince them that they can make a lot of money if they place their courses on the Web.[28] Of course, these same companies profit by selling software and equipment to universities, and these joint ventures often fail to live up to the promise of increased profits. Moreover, as I argued in *Integrating Hypertextual Subjects: Computers, Composition, and Academic Labor*, the more of its courses that a university places online, the less it is able to distinguish itself from for-profit online rivals. One of the main reasons why students go to prestigious research universities is that they want to interact with famous professors and other smart students, but these opportunities are lost in many forms of online education. Thus, a university that relies on distance education ends up losing its prestige and value.

In many ways, universities' habitual use of large lecture classes already makes their instruction very distant. After all, what is the difference between watching a lecture on a computer screen and sitting in a room with eight hundred other students? In both cases, there is very little interaction between the students and the professor, and in both cases, the students are virtually invisible, while they consume information in a passive manner. However, anyone who cares about the quality of higher education should understand that the solution is not to use more technology to make big classes seem smaller or put classes online. Rather, the solution is to insist on having more small, interactive classes in which students become active members of their educational communities. Some would say this would cost too much money, but I have shown above that it can cost more money to have large lecture classes because they involve a high price for the sections taught by graduate students.

Murray Sperber argues in *Beer and Circus* that universities do know what a quality education is because whenever they advertise their honors programs, they always stress the fact that students are taught in small seminars led by expert teachers.[29] Honors programs also proclaim that their classes for the select few rely on a form of education that is interactive and inquisitive, not on the standardized testing of memorized information. As I will argue in the next chapter, parents and students need to push for this type of education, but we must first force universities to take their core mission seriously.

9

Making All Public
Higher Education Free

Throughout this book, I have pointed out a series of counterintuitive paradoxes. It seems that the more money research universities spend, the higher their tuition and the lower their quality of instruction. One would think that raising the price would improve the education, but as I have shown, due to the lack of concern for instructional quality, that is not the case. Moreover, research universities now often function like investment banks, and one of their central concerns is to drive down labor costs while they increase the compensation of administrators and star faculty. I have also argued that one reason why students generally do not complain about the state of their education is that universities spend a great deal of money pleasing them outside of the classroom. Instead of simply bemoaning this situation, I want to discuss several of the ways we can improve the quality of education at universities as we control costs and increase access.

Free Public Higher Education

In the 1960s only a small percentage of Finnish students completed high school, and Finland ranked in the middle of developed countries on international test scores. Forty years later, Finland had one of the highest percentages of high-school graduates in the world, and its students had the highest test scores in math and science. Many people have asked how Finland achieved this transformation, and can we apply this model to other systems of education. According to Pasi Sahlberg's *Finnish Lessons*, there were five major components to Finland's success: (1) all education became public and free; (2) teachers became well compensated and highly trained; (3) education became interactive and experienced based; (4) students at an early age received individual attention; and (5) in high school, students were able to choose if they wanted to pursue a vocational track or an academic track.[1] It is my contention that we can apply to higher education in America many of the same educational reforms that were used in K–12 education in Finland.

The first step in this process is to calculate how much it would cost to make all public higher education free in the United States. In 2008–9, there were 6.4 million full-time-equivalent undergraduate students enrolled in public universities and 4.3 million enrolled in community colleges.[2] In 2009–10, the average cost of tuition, room, and board for undergraduates at public four-year institutions was $14,870; at two-year public colleges, it was $7,629.[3] If we multiply the number of students in each segment of public higher education by the average total cost, we discover that the cost of making all public universities free would have been $95 billion in 2009–10, with an annual cost of $33 billion for all community colleges—or a total of $128 billion.

While $128 billion seems like a large figure, we need to remember that in 2010, the federal government spent $35 billion on Pell grants and $104 billion on student loans, while the states spent at least $10 billion on financial aid for universities and colleges and another $76 billion for direct support of higher education.[4] Furthermore, looking at various state and federal tax breaks and deductions for tuition, it might be possible to make all public higher education free by just using current resources in a more effective manner. And as I have argued throughout this book, the cost for free public higher education could be greatly reduced by lowering the spending on administration, athletics, housing, dining, amenities, research, and graduate education.[5]

It is important to stress that the current tuition rates are inflated because schools increase their sticker price in order to subsidize institutional financial aid for low-income students and to provide merit aid for wealthy, high-scoring students. If we eliminated the current aid system and each school instead received a set amount of money for each student from the state and federal governments, we could significantly reduce the cost of making public higher education free in America. Also, by eliminating the need for student loans, the government would save billions of dollars by avoiding the current cost of nonpayment of loans, servicing and subsidizing them, and borrowers' defaults.

Rather than directly funding public higher education institutions, state and federal governments have often relied on tax deductions and credits to support individual students. The tax code has been used to fund higher education because it is easier for Congress to pass a tax break than it is to get funding for a particular program, but what this system has achieved is a tremendous subsidy for upper-middle-class and wealthy families, while lower-income students are forced to take out huge loans to pay for their education. According to a recent study, "From 1999 to 2009, the government spent $70 billion on tax breaks aimed at subsidizing higher education for families . . . about 13 percent, or $9.4 billion, of that total went to families making more than $100,000 a year. At the same time, only 11 percent went to the neediest families, those making less than $25,000. Families in the middle—those making between $25,000 and $99,999—received the lion's share of the aid, taking in slightly more than three-quarters of the benefits."[6]

Later the report indicates that more of the funding now goes to the wealthiest Americans: "Nearly 83 percent of the higher education tax benefits distributed from 1999 to 2001 went to families earning less than $75,000 per year. No benefits went to those earning more than $100,000. By contrast, in the last three tax years alone, families making between $100,000 and $180,000 received nearly a quarter of the benefits. The share going to middle-income families sharply declined."[7] This tax system for higher education is a great example of how so many of our governmental policies end up subsidizing the wealthy while poor and middle-class citizens pay more and get less.

In 2010–11, the federal government provided the following tax subsidies, breaks, and credits for higher education: student interest rate exemption ($1.4 billion); exclusion from taxation of employer-provided educational assistance ($1.1 billion); exclusion of interest on student-loan bonds ($0.6 billion); exclusion of scholarship and fellowship income ($3.0 billion); exclusion of earnings of qualified tuition programs—savings account programs ($0.6 billion): the HOPE tax credit ($5.4 billion); the

Lifetime Learning tax credit ($5.5 billion); parental personal exemption for students age nineteen or over ($3.4 billion); and state prepaid tuition plans ($1.8 billion).[8] There's also the stimulus package's American Opportunity Tax Credit ($14.4 billion) and the part of the deductibility of charitable contributions for gifts to educational institutions ($4.9 billion). In total, the federal government lost over $40 billion in tax revenue due to higher education in 2010.

If we made all public higher education free, not only could we do away with this unjust tax system, but we could also stop the movement of public funds to expensive private and for-profit universities and colleges. What most people do not realize is that the use of financial aid and tax subsidies for individual students has resulted in a system where much of the governmental support for higher education ends up going to private institutions that cater to the super-rich or to low-achieving for-profit schools. In fact, during a 2012 congressional investigation of for-profit colleges, it was discovered that up to a quarter of all federal Pell grant money is now going to these corporate schools, which charge a high tuition and graduate very few students.[9] What this investigation did not uncover, however, was the total amount of state and federal tax breaks that go to support for-profit institutions.

There has been recent research on how much the federal government has spent on tax deductions and credits for higher education, but as far as I can tell, no one has examined how much states are spending on these tax breaks for colleges and universities. However, it is safe to estimate that the total subsidy by the states is at least the same as the total federal level of support. This is because many of the states have tax deductions that exceed the national tax breaks for tuition, and most states have tax-advantaged 529 college savings plans.[10] For example, in New York State, the tuition tax credit goes up to $5,000 per year per student, and the tuition tax deduction is $10,000 for each eligible student.[11] It is important to note that tax deductions favor the wealthy because many low-income families pay little if any income taxes.

One of the great secrets in higher education funding is the role played by 529 college savings plans: "In 2000 a total of $2.6 billion was invested in 529 plans. This grew to $14 billion in 2001 and more than $92 billion in mid-2006. The student aid resource *Finaid.org* projects that total investment in 529 plans will reach $175 billion to $250 billion by 2010, with a total of 10 million to 15 million accounts opened."[12] Not only do state governments lose billions of dollars in tax revenue each year due to these 529 plans, but the wealthy have figured out how to use these plans as all-purpose tax shelters. For example, if a couple puts $26,000 a year for each child into an account and decides later to use the money to buy a yacht instead, only the investment gains will be assessed a 10 percent penalty and taxed as income. Also, contributions made to a 529 are removed from a family's estate, and 529 plan owners can name a successor to the account when they die, which enables the plans to shelter money for multiple generations.

One way that wealthy people use these accounts to avoid paying taxes is by giving each other gifts. Gift taxes can be avoided if contributions into the plans over a five-year period do not exceed $65,000 for single taxpayers and $130,000 for married couples. Clearly, it is only the wealthiest Americans who are able to profit from this type of plan. In fact, according to a Department of the Treasury report, "Currently there are effectively no limits on Section 529 account balances. Because 43 states offer plans open to residents in other states, a beneficiary can have accounts in as many as 44 states, each state with a limit exceeding $224,465."[13] It is obvious that only wealthy people can afford to save and invest this type of money. Moreover, the same study of 529 plans details how the richest families are using these plans for tax shelters:

> Data from the 2007 Survey of Consumer Finance found that among households in the top five percent of income—average income, $548,000 per year—those with education savings plans held an average balance of $106,250. That's more than triple the average for households in the 90th–95th percentile, more than ten times the balance for the 50th–75th percentile, etc. Second, among households in Kansas who took a state income tax deduction for 529 contributions, the average deduction for households making over $250,000 per year was $10,323. For those in the $100K–$250K range it was less than $5,000, for everyone else, less than $3,000.[14]

As this federal government report indicates, 529 plans have now become an effective way to subsidize wealthy people; meanwhile, states are being forced to cut their higher education budgets due to their lack of tax revenue.

If we took all of the state and federal money that is lost each year due to these tax credits, deductions, and shelters, we could make public higher education free for millions of Americans. However, the tax code is rigged to provide aid to wealthy people, and one side effect of this system is that private universities are able to charge higher tuition because they know that the parents of many of the incoming students will pay only a fraction of the full price thanks to merit aid, institutional aid, and tax breaks. Furthermore, once the private universities increase their tuition, they raise the bar for everyone else, making tuition increases at public universities appear more tolerable. And since the top public universities compete with the top private universities for star faculty and administrators, the more the private institutions are able to increase their tuition, the more the public ones have to pay their star faculty.

To contain rising tuition at private universities and the subsidization of high-cost, low-value for-profit schools, the government needs to move away from the current emphasis on tax breaks and tax shelters, which can be accomplished in part by making all public higher education free. Replacing the current mix of financial aid, institutional aid, tax subsidies, and grants with direct funding for public institutions would give the government a way to control costs at both public and private universities and colleges. The federal government could also require states to maintain their funding for public institutions in return for increased federal support, and once we stabilize funding and make higher education free, there will be no need for so many students and institutions to go into debt.

Why Make Public Higher Education Free?

The central reason why we should change how we support public higher education and make it free is that this system plays a key role in allowing us to have an effective democracy. Thomas Jefferson argued for a free public university because he knew that in order to have a real democracy, you need to have highly educated citizens. Jefferson proclaimed that "it is safer to have the whole people respectably enlightened than a few in a high state of science and the many in ignorance."[15] Jefferson wanted the United States to avoid the aristocracy and tyranny he saw in Europe, and in his 1818 report to the commissioners of the University of Virginia, he

proclaimed that public universities were necessary "to develop the reasoning faculties of our youth, enlarge their minds, cultivate their morals,
and instill into them the precepts of virtue and order; to enlighten them
with mathematical and physical sciences, which advance the arts and
administer to the health, the subsistence and comforts of human life;
and, generally, to form them to habits of reflection and correct action,
rendering them examples of virtue to others and of happiness within
themselves."[16] It is interesting to note that Jefferson did not say that the
main goal of higher education was to prepare students for future jobs;
rather, he rightly believed that universities need to cater to the whole
person by helping students develop better reasoning skills, form moral
attitudes, and become happier.

As I have argued throughout this book, these broad goals for higher
education are being undermined by the high cost of tuition and related
expenses that drive students to go into debt and force them to focus on
pursuing a high-paying job to pay off their high student loans. Furthermore, universities themselves are now stressing that the major advantage
of going to college is that people will earn more, and the unintended effect
of this argument is that higher education is seen as a private good purchased by an individual student. This leads states to conclude that they
can cut their funding for universities, letting the responsibility for paying
the increased costs fall on the individual student—who is seen as making a
down payment on a future job.

The current system has also increased wealth inequality in the country by motivating public universities and colleges to accept students who
can pay the full bill or who get large aid packages due to their high SAT
scores. As we have seen, one result is that the best public universities are
reducing their number of low-income and minority students in order to
chase after wealthy American students and foreign students who pay full
tuition without financial aid. If we leave the current system unchecked,
we will only increase the growing inequality in American society. Recent
research has shown that unequal educational attainment goes hand and
hand with income inequality, as well as with higher rates of crime and
lower health standards.[17] In other words, the more public higher education
becomes privatized, the more it becomes unequal—and the more society
in general suffers.

Universities have been privatized because they no longer serve a public mission; instead, they often operate like large corporations. In this type of corporate university, administrators with little or no training in education run schools as if the goal was to increase compensation for the people at the top, while the vast majority of the teachers and workers are paid poverty-level wages. A small minority of star faculty negotiate private deals for higher compensation and lower course loads, while the rest of the professors are left doing more and earning less. These private deals not only create collusion between professors and administrators, but they also undermine the entire notion of a public institution centered on transparency and a shared mission.

Another privatizing factor in higher education is the move to online classes, where students are seen simply as isolated individuals paying a fee to access university courses. Not only are these students usually studying and learning alone, but they are also socialized to see education as a consumer product, something that is purchased by private individuals in a private transaction. Although for-profit colleges are an extreme example of this type of privatization, public universities are adopting many of these same educational strategies that for-profit schools use. Just as the for-profits downsize the roles of faculty members by eliminating tenure and academic freedom and imposing a prescribed curriculum, public universities and colleges are replacing tenured positions with part-time faculty who have little if any rights and receive reduced rates of compensation and benefits. The only way to stop this privatization of our public institutions is the make all public higher education free and to stabilize the academic labor force, while increasing the transparency of how universities and colleges spend their money.

The Educational Reasons for Free Higher Education

Making public higher education free would have several important effects. It would allow more students to attain degrees, because the biggest reason why students drop out of colleges and universities is that they cannot afford the high cost of continuing. Moreover, many students who do not drop out nonetheless fail to graduate in a timely fashion because they spend so much time working in order to afford the increasing costs of tuition and room and board.[18] If public higher education were free, students could stay in school and graduate on time, and decreasing the average time to graduate would allow more students to get college degrees.

Free public higher education could also lead to improvements in the working conditions of the vast majority of faculty who now teach undergraduate courses. One way this could happen would be to greatly reduce the number of graduate students teaching undergraduate classes, which would increase the demand for new teachers. And if the federal government required that most of undergraduate courses be taught by full-time faculty, we could stabilize the academic job market and concentrate on rewarding undergraduate faculty who focus on providing quality instruction.

To both control costs and increase instructional quality, the government could make sure that every student is taught in a small class by an expert teacher who has academic freedom and job security. In fact we could teach every undergraduate student at American public universities and colleges in classes of no more than twenty-five students for a direct instructional cost of under $5,000 per student per year. I arrived at these figures by extrapolating salary and course-load data from the University of California in the following way. Currently 75 percent of all courses in US higher education are taught by non-tenure-track faculty, and in the UC system, these teachers receive on average $62,000 to teach six courses a year. If we add benefits (15 percent of salary) to this total, and each course has twenty-five students, the cost per student for each class is $475. In the case of tenured faculty, if the average salary with benefits is $100,000 and the average annual course load is four courses for professors who teach undergraduate courses, the total cost per course per student is $1,000. So if the average student takes eight courses in a year, and six of the courses are taught by nonprofessors, the total cost would be $4,850.

The reason why I am using the University of California as the basis for my calculations is that this system is known to have the best contract and compensation structure for non-tenure-track faculty in the United States. Thus, while many adjunct and part-time teachers in America are paid only about $3,000 a course and have no benefits, my proposed model would increase the pay and job security for most of the teachers in US higher education—yet it would be less expensive than the current haphazard use of graduate students, part-time teachers, and research professors.[19]

In fact, if the direct instructional cost per student were $4,850, we would be able to reduce the total costs to educate each student while simultaneously improving instruction through the use of small, interactive leaning environments.

As the experience in Finland shows, a key to improving the quality of education is to increase the respect and compensation for teachers. It might seem that this would drive up the costs of higher education, but we could actually save money by regularizing the use of non-tenure-track teachers and reducing noneducational expenses. Because the majority of people teaching undergraduates today lack tenure, what we need to do is to stabilize their jobs by moving people into full-time positions. That would cut down on faculty turnover and the need to hire and manage a stream of part-time teachers constantly moving through the revolving door. Furthermore, by allowing these newly full-time faculty members to participate in faculty senates and serve on departmental committees, the current high amount of service required from professors could be reduced. All faculty would then have time to take on tasks like student advising that are now done by an army of staff, which would result in significant savings.

If the majority of the faculty teaching undergraduate students were hired and promoted based on their teaching ability, we could improve instruction and contain costs, but it would be necessary to involve accreditors in the peer review of instructional faculty, as I discuss in the next chapter. The best way to improve educational quality is not, as some have argued, to make students take standardized tests; rather, we should be making sure that the teachers are teaching in an effective manner. As I will argue, we already have a model for this in the University of California system.

Dividing the Faculty

Inherent in the new structure I am proposing is the idea that one way to improve instruction and decrease costs is to recognize that some researchers should only do research, and some teachers should only teach. Therefore, I recommend that universities and colleges establish three types of professors: teaching professors, research professors, and hybrid professors. If we stop forcing research professors into the classroom, we will be able to allow them to concentrate on what they do best and avoid what they often do in an ineffective manner. In contrast, the current system—in which states and students pay for expensive research professors to teach—drives up the cost of instruction and allows people who have a proven record of being ineffective teachers to continue to lower the quality of instruction. For research professors, we should continue the current incentive system at research universities, which privileges research over teaching. But we should get rid of the false myth that research and teaching always go hand in hand.

If we allow researchers to be rewarded for what they do best, we should also provide incentives for teachers to concentrate on instruction. By providing job security for the people who do most of the teaching at research universities, we can make undergraduate instruction an important priority.[20] Key to this transformation is establishing shared methods of assessing teaching, and this means not placing so much emphasis on student evaluations to reward and promote teachers. Instead, we need to enhance the peer review of instruction in order to make student learning and quality instruction the center of American research universities.

How to Rate and Rank Universities

To motivate research universities to put their money and effort into undergraduate instruction, we have to transform how schools are currently being rated and ranked. Instead of relying on the SAT scores of incoming students to evaluate universities and colleges, we should require these institutions to report the number of student credit hours earned in classes with fewer than twenty-six students and the percentage of their budgets that go to direct instructional costs. These statistics would motivate schools to educate students in small classes taught by faculty with secure jobs. Related to these changes in the ranking and rating of schools could be a federal investigation into the accuracy and value of the statistics reported in books like the U.S. News & World Report Best Colleges 2012. As I have pointed out, when schools report on the percentage of faculty who are full-time, they often count only the professors, even though 75 percent of the courses are taught by nonprofessors. Instead, schools should report on the percentage of student credit hours taught by full-time faculty.[21]

This emphasis on class size and full-time faculty in the ranking of universities could turn the current incentive system upside down and would force universities to be more accountable to their instructional missions. If instruction, not just research, became the key to a university's reputation, these institutions would be motivated to put more money into instruction, which would reverse the current practice of using tuition dollars to subsidize sponsored research and administration. After all, what often makes educational costs go up at research universities is that students and taxpayers are forced to pay for the escalating salaries of graduate and professional school professors and administrators who often have no connection to undergraduate instruction. Some people might object that by splitting research off from instruction, I am losing the whole point of going to a research university. However, I have shown that the research mission is often subsidized by the instructional budget, and there is no proof that a good researcher will make a good teacher; in fact, the opposite is sometimes the case. I have also argued that we should develop a third group of professors, the hybrids, who will be judged equally for their research and their teaching. Once teaching becomes a priority, and we motivate schools to rely on small, interactive classes taught by expert teachers, we can dramatically improve the quality of undergraduate education. By reducing the number of large classes, we will also be able to reduce the number of standardized multiple-choice exams and PowerPoint lecturers.

To help motivate research universities make some of these changes, the federal government should hold these institutions accountable by making sure that they report on their costs and spending in a clear and transparent fashion. As I have argued throughout this book, if university budgets and priorities became more transparent, we would be able to see why costs go up and quality goes down. For instance, a careful accounting of money spent on technology would show that supposedly cost-saving initiatives usually end up costing more money instead. It would also demonstrate that although universities often use student tuition and state funds to support research projects, when these projects turn a profit, the added revenue rarely finds its way back into the classroom.

The only way, then, to really improve the quality of education at American universities is to make sure that these institutions make learning a priority, and this transformation would entail changing how schools spend their money. However, even if universities decide to dedicate more of their funds to instruction, little will change if students continue to see higher education as merely a way of gathering grades that they can use to go to graduate school or get a high-paying job. Thus, one of the biggest challenges facing higher education is how to get students to care about what they learn, not just what grades they earn. We need a shift in cultural attitudes: too many parents think that if they do not stress the importance of grades and scores on high-stake tests when their children are young, later in life the children will be denied important opportunities. However, many studies show that when students are motivated only by external rewards and praise, they are unable to learn when they encounter failure or difficulties.[22] If we had more small, interactive classes whose teachers valued what students actually thought and said, we could move away from the cultural obsession with grades. And if students did not have to go into debt in order to pursue a degree, they would be less likely to see undergraduate education as only a means to a high-paying job.

For all of the problems I have been discussing, insisting on quality education is the key to the solution. But what is quality education? Can people agree on a definition? I believe that teachers and students often know good instruction when they see it, and that one of its characteristics is that active participation in the formation and questioning of knowledge. In other words, instead of having students simply memorize information for standardized tests, teachers have to engage students in a process where knowledge is interrogated and created.[23] In large lecture classes, which are now the staple of research universities, this type of interactive education is often very hard to achieve, which is why we must insist that class size is important.

Beyond Universities of Debt

By tying free public education to an emphasis on high-quality instruction, we can reduce costs and motivate schools to concentrate on their core missions. Moreover, in eliminating the need for students to take out huge loans, we can end the current economic model, which creates a type of indentured servitude. In the current system, many students cannot find a job after they graduate, or they are able to find only low-paying, part-time employment. Even though they have very little income, they have to start paying off their student loans. This means that they start their working lives as slaves to debt, and their decisions become controlled by their need to pay for their past education. Student loans cannot be forgiven through bankruptcy, and if borrowers miss payments or go into default, they are charged huge penalties. The government can even garnish their wages and withhold their tax refunds if they borrowed money through a federal loan program. Thus, instead of higher education leading to greater income and social mobility, it often leads to greater social and economic inequality. It is unclear why more students do not protest the fact that as they pay more for a shortchanged education, they commit themselves to a life of debt.

Perhaps one reason why so many of them accept this situation is that their education has taught them to be passive consumers, competing for scarce resources (first grades, and later jobs). In other words, just as debt serves to discipline students and punish them for their past expenses, education socializes students to be silent and passive. This silencing of students is coupled with the silencing of faculty, most of whom now work without job security or academic freedom. And on the rare occasions when students and the faculty do not remain silent, there are always the campus police—who have increasingly clamped down on any protests at American universities. In many ways, the police stand as the last line of discipline in the age of austerity. After all, most of the students protesting the high cost of tuition are doing so because state budgets for higher education have been reduced. Thus, when students protest against tuition increases, they are also protesting against the state. As governments impose reductions on public programs, students become both the victims and the symbols of a system that has turned its back on the basic function of educating its youth.

By moving away from free public higher education, America has undermined its own democracy and economy. Not only are students trapped in a cycle of debt as they pay more and get less, but the people teaching the students are increasingly left without job security or a livable wage. Meanwhile, universities are using an unstable economy and reduced state funding as a permanent crisis that justifies laying off faculty, reducing workers' benefits, and scaring teachers into a state of complacency and cynicism. This disciplining of the faculty is coupled with the production of an army of surplus teachers whose presence drives down wages and prevents academic laborers from forming unions or engaging in other collective actions.

As I will argue in the final chapter, our public higher education system can be improved if we not only make it free, but also change the way we teach students and value teachers. As the example of Finland shows, education becomes effective if everyone has an equal opportunity to pursue it, and every student receives personal attention and guidance. This does not mean that every young person in America should go to college; in fact, we need to recognize the multiple forms of education and training that currently exist in our country. However, all students who want to pursue public higher education should be given the opportunity to do so without having to take on life-crippling levels of debt.

10

Educating Students for a Multicultural Democracy

Currently, there are two major movements in education around the globe: increased stress on efficiency and standardized testing, and a growing focus on teaching the whole student and covering a large variety of subject matter. Driving much of the first movement is the idea that education's only purpose is to prepare a student for a future job in knowledge economy; the second movement is centered on helping students become better citizens and thinkers. In the case of higher education, extreme examples of these two movements can be found in for-profit online universities and non-profit honors colleges. Students at for-profits pay high fees, usually with the help of government grants, to receive an inferior education provided by an army of underpaid adjuncts. These high-paying students rarely graduate, and the few of them who do earn a degree or certificate typically have huge amounts of debt. Furthermore, even though their programs are usually centered on job training, most of the students are unable to find employment. In contrast, students at honors colleges at public universities take a wide variety of courses, which are usually taught in small seminars by expert teachers.

The two extremes I have depicted here represent the central choice that we need to make as a multicultural democracy in a globalized economy. Although it is tempting to assess universities by looking at how their students do on standardized tests, Pasi Sahlberg argues that Finland was able to rise to the top in international tests by not stressing standardized tests in its educational system.[1] Instead, Finland concentrated on making public education free and giving teachers the tools and respect they needed to be effective instructors. A key aspect of this type of education is the recognition that standardized tests not only affect what and how students learn but also what and how instructors teach. When they must teach to the test, educators are motivated to provide instruction in an uncritical and rote manner that makes them set aside their passion for teaching and limits their ability to teach the whole student. In contrast to this standardized system, Sahlberg argues that all educators must learn how to teach every student and prepare all of them for the new types of knowledge that are required in an ever-changing and unpredictable knowledge economy.[2] Thus, instead of making the students and the teachers unhappy by forcing them to concentrate on memorizing information, educators in Finland have committed themselves to an interactive and holistic model of instruction.

A key aspect of the Finnish system is the idea that teachers need to be respected and given the freedom to teach to their strengths. However, if we look at teaching at American universities and colleges, we discover that the vast majority of the instructors are part-time faculty and graduate students who have neither academic freedom nor job security; thus, the system itself does not treat these educators with respect. Also, even the professors who are generally respected by society are rarely taught how to be effective teachers or how contemporary students learn. As Howard Gardner has argued, most schools concentrate on a single form of intelligence, and they fail to teach emotional or social intelligence.[3] In other words, students should not only memorize facts and theories, but also learn about how they and others perceive the world on an emotional and social basis.

Ironically, Sahlberg reveals that Finnish educators have learned from American education theorists how to teach in an effective manner by incorporating a more comprehensive understanding of student learning. A key aspect to this Finnish model is the use of empirical and theoretical studies to ground teaching in proven methods. Yet, as I have pointed out throughout this book, American professors rarely study the research on teaching and learning that their own institutions produce. And although most of the recent breakthroughs in neuroscience and cognitive science concerning how people learn and think have been developed at research universities, these important findings rarely make their way into the university classroom. Part of the problem here is that there has been an almost complete separation between undergraduate and graduate education. Large undergraduate classes are still using older models of teaching and thinking, even though small graduate courses often incorporate a more participatory model of instruction and research.

It is clear that undergraduate courses have to be updated, and this does not mean only limiting the use of large lecture classes and multiple-choice exams. In addition, universities need to pay more careful attention to students' writing, thinking, and social interactions. Sadly, when students do write in their large lecture classes, they usually receive very little feedback because no one has the time to carefully read and comment on the huge numbers of papers generated in a large class. Students learn from this experience that the system does not care about their ideas, so they quickly limit their own thinking. In contrast, by not stressing testing in its classes, Finland has developed a mostly fear-free system of education.[4] Since students taking tests often experience a high level of anxiety, the reduction of testing increases the mental health of the students, which is one way the Finnish system caters to the whole student. Also, by not emphasizing standardized tests, this system is able to focus students on internal motivations rather than external rewards. Students learn not only how to be more independent, but also how to trust their own thinking and creativity.

Finnish educators discovered that the best way to educate all students—not just the top ones—is to make education free and give individual students the attention they need. Applying this approach to US higher education might seem like a costly proposition, but in the previous chapter, I demonstrated that it could be done without costing the government or taxpayers much additional money if current resources were used in a more thoughtful and systemic manner. However, to transform our system of higher education, we must follow Finland's path to educational excellence by starting with the principle that every student should be given an equal opportunity to learn. In fact, inspired in part by the work of the American educator John Dewey, Finland realized that every class is a microcosm of the larger society: if you want a democratic society, you need democratic learning environments.[5] This not only means affirming that all students are capable of learning, but it also requires allowing students to actively participate in their classes.

As we have seen, in many large lecture classes using multiple-choice exams, the teacher becomes the sole voice and authority in the class, which causes students to internalize the message that their own views and knowledge do not count. This is a highly antidemocratic model of education, and it trains students to be passive, fearful citizens. In contrast, when Finnish schools test their students, most of the exams are essay-based, with open-ended questions that allow for the maximum amount of student thinking and creativity.[6] Sahlberg argues that at the same time that Finland was starting to base its educational methods on cognitive and neuroscientific findings from the United States, other developed countries, including America, were moving to a system of standardized testing and for-profit education. The use of standardized tests to judge teachers, students, and schools has resulted in a culture of fear in many schools, and the result has been a decrease in learning and achievement, as registered by global literacy exams.[7]

It should be clear that the best way to improve instruction is not to stress standardized testing, but if universities and colleges follow current trends in K–12 education, we may see the adoption of this highly destructive educational method at these institutions. Although our current ranking and rating systems are deeply flawed, as I have shown, we should not think that the only alternative is to use high-stakes tests to evaluate higher education. Even more holistic types of testing, like the College Learning Assessment, could result in teachers teaching to the test and students learning how to game the system. Following the Finnish model, we must resist the claim that the only way to help students and schools improve is to hold them to high testing standards. Many school reformers in the United States have good intentions, but they often do not understand how students learn and how effective instructors teach. In fact, one of the major results of the No Child Left Behind Act and other national policies based on testing was that many teachers left the profession. Another was that public schools became increasingly segregated because growing numbers of wealthier parents—most of whom were white—put their children in private schools instead.[8]

How to Evaluate Teachers in Higher Education

If something like No Child Left Behind was brought to higher education in America, our colleges and universities would become even more segregated and ineffective than they are now. If you want to have a truly democratic system of education, it is simply wrong to evaluate teachers and schools on the abilities of their students. Rather, we must evaluate the ability of teachers to teach in an effective manner, but this should not be done in some alienating and standardized way. As my experience in the University of California system has shown me, the highest rated teachers are often the untenured faculty who are evaluated by their skills at communicating effectively and including students in the learning process. Because the union contract regulating these teachers bases promotion on peer review of the instructors, there is a great incentive for teachers to focus on excellent teaching.[9] The contract requires that each instructor be evaluated according to the following criteria: (1) command of the subject matter and continued growth in mastering new topics; (2) ability to organize and present course materials; (3) ability to awaken in students an awareness of the importance of the subject matter; (4) ability to arouse curiosity in beginning students and to stimulate advanced students to do creative work; and (5) achievements of students in their field. These criteria are rather broad, but they do get to the heart of what we expect university teachers to be able to do. Not only is it important for excellent teachers to be able to present their course material in an effective manner, but good instructors also motivate their students to participate actively in their education by allowing students to develop their own projects and skills.

One problem with this peer review system of faculty teaching is that reviewers from the instructors' home department may have an incentive to give their fellow teachers a good evaluation, and this is why it is necessary to involve external accreditors in the peer review process. Accrediting agencies have as part of their mandate to examine the quality of undergraduate instruction, but in my experience, they rely almost exclusively on reports about this from the institutions they are examining. In fact, during a recent accreditation visit at UCLA, I asked the accreditors how they know that the professors are teaching in an effective manner. They told me not to worry because they know that UCLA is a great learning institution, and when I pressed them, they informed me that their mission is to make sure we have the proper self-assessment tools in place. My conclusion was that these accreditors were not interested in examining the effectiveness of undergraduate education in any serious manner.

One way that universities and accreditors could monitor the teaching done in higher education would be to videotape classes and have experts examine the quality of education. Although this may seem like a costly and intrusive type of educational control, many universities already record many of their classes in order to put them online, and some universities have already begun using recorded classes to study teaching. For example, Harvard recently decided that it needs to improve undergraduate instruction, and it has suggested videotaping the classes of many of its professors so it can see if teachers are actually teaching in an effective manner.[10] If accreditors insisted that all universities record classes from every course, an effective peer review system could be established that would be much better than the current system of relying on student evaluations and occasional visits from possibly biased colleagues.

Although we need to develop a culture of teaching connected to a concern for student learning, we should resist the temptation to turn to easy-to-grade standardized exams for this purpose. As Sahlberg stresses in his analysis of Finnish schools, instructor and school autonomy is an essential aspect of building a respect for teaching and learning, but there still needs to be some method of quality control.[11] Furthermore, instead of seeing university teaching as an individual activity, faculty members need to view instruction as a shared process that involves a community of scholars. Part of this change can be motivated by funding professional development for instructors to learn more about contemporary teaching methods, but universities and colleges should develop their own additional ways of emphasizing high-quality undergraduate instruction.

It is important to note that in Finland, almost all of the teachers are unionized, and they share a union with staff and administrators. It is hard to imagine establishing this type of system in the United States, but what we are seeing in America is that as the number of teachers without tenure increases, more of them are joining unions to protect their wages and jobs. If this trend continues, unions will be able to play a major role in pushing for high-quality instruction, ensuring that enough money is being spent on undergraduate education and that hiring and promoting faculty members is based on their ability to teach in an effective manner. Furthermore, the quality of instruction can be improved as instructors are given the time and resources (including offices, computers, and professional development funds) to improve their teaching methods. However, one union has already agreed to a system of rewarding teachers for improving their students' scores on standardized tests, and more unions are being pressured to connect faculty pay to students' scores—a trend we must resist.[12] Not only does this type of system force teachers to teach to the test, but it also gives them too many incentives to cheat and creates a destructive culture of competition.

One of the underlying messages from the educational reform movement in Finland is that in a culture of educational competition, everyone loses. Not only are the teachers forced to turn education into a high-stakes routine, but the students also see their education narrowed. Instead of competition, Finland stresses cooperation, and this emphasis has profound educational and social effects. When students no longer think that all that matters is to outscore other students on standardized tests, they begin to respect and value the ideas of the people around them. Also, when you move from an educational system based on competition to one based on cooperation, the teachers are motivated to work together and share their ideas about what works and what doesn't in the classroom. Ultimately, a system based on cooperation trains students to respect others and value their own democracy.

Nonprofit Teaching in a Multicultural Democracy

In *Not for Profit*, Martha Nussbaum argues that a key to teaching students in a multicultural democracy and a cooperative educational environment is to help them develop empathic understanding. In other words, instead of focusing on standardized tests and memorized information, universities have to combine instruction in math and science with more humanistic approaches to mental cognition. From her perspective, a major contribution of the humanities to learning is that literature and art classes help students to think about how other cultures and people experience the world. Unfortunately, universities and colleges are following the trend in K–12 schools, and they have cut classes in the humanities in order to concentrate on the subjects that are assessed on standardized tests and are supposed to lead to jobs in the knowledge economy. Thus, in the race to quantify student learning, the classes that are harder to evaluate have lost their funding.

Nussbaum argues that the current global push for standardized testing and for-profit education does not prepare students to play a role in a multicultural democracy. She claims that if current global educational trends continue, "nations all over the world will soon be producing generations of useful machines, rather than complete citizens who can think for themselves, criticize tradition, and understand the significance of another person's sufferings and achievements."[13] Nussbaum stresses that due to the emphasis on standardized testing for science and math in K–12 education, students enter higher education with a very limited idea of what it means to learn and understand the world around them.

According to Nussbaum, the use of large lecture classes at research universities not only blocks the democratic participation of students in their own education, but it also does not train undergraduates to "argue for themselves, rather than defer to traditional authority."[14] From this perspective, our supposedly liberal institutions are actually highly conservative, and even though most professors may identify themselves as progressive and moderate, the way they teach their courses often functions to reinforce a conservative mind-set. This political conflict between how professors teach and what they are teaching reflects the fact that many faculty members have not been taught how students learn or what are the best ways to teach people today. In order to correct this problem, professors and instructors need to look at what neuroscience and cognitive science tell us about thinking and learning.

The Conservative Brain

Recent studies in neuroscience have shown that various parts of our brains process information in different ways.[15] These studies reveal that sections of the right part of our brain tend to process experiences in a fast, intuitive way, while the left side tends to utilize the slow process of conscious reasoning.[16] For example, in *The Master and His Emissary*, Ian McGilchrist stresses that a key transition in Western culture is the shift from an emphasis on the right brain's use of intuition, empathy, and emotions to the left brain's stress on logic, reason, and abstraction. According to McGilchrist, the left half of the brain uses abstract systems, while the right half locates every experience in an immediate context.[17]

We should not put too much emphasis on a strict opposition between the left and right brain, but this distinction is helpful because it points to the different ways that the mind processes information. Moreover, the terms "left brain" and "right brain" can be read as broad areas that may not be completely localized in specific parts of the brain; in fact, much recent neuroscience research sees the brain as an integrated network, with mental functions handled by a series of different brain areas. Also, by using the term "brain" instead of "mind," we are emphasizing the role of biological systems in mental structures, although current research shows that biology, psychology, and social influences are constantly intermixing. We should understand the terms "left brain" and "right brain" as generalized metaphors for different biosocial processes.

In terms of education, because sections of the left part of the brain are dedicated to placing experiences and thoughts in a logical, sequential order, it is mostly this part of the brain that is tested in standardized exams and multiple-choice tests. Most university professors actually teach as if students have only half a brain—the half that is dominated by the left side's preference for abstraction, logic, and sequential order. One could even argue that the entire foundation of the modern Western university is predicated on the dominance of the left brain and the exclusion of the right side of our thinking.

Like liberal politicians who think that all you have to do to get a voter to support a new policy is to explain the logical reasons behind it, liberal professors tend to believe that reason—not emotion—is the main content of our minds and the key to education.[18] However, neuroscientists have discovered that many people first make an intuitive decision in the right parts of their brain, and then they use the left parts to rationalize their choice after the fact.[19] The lesson for politicians and educators is not that we should give up on reason; rather, we need to cater to both sides of the brain, and the best way to do this is to create a conscious dialogue between emotions and reason.

This need for a greater left-brain awareness of right-brain functioning has been made persuasively in such books as Malcolm Gladwell's *Blink* and Jonah Lehrer's *How We Decide*, but these theories have rarely made their way into university teaching. Thus, a great paradox is that although many professors teach in a highly logical left-brain way, they believe intuitively that the only way to learn how to teach is to copy the style and methods of their own teachers. In other words, they end up teaching as if students learn only with their left brains, but they themselves believe that the best way to learn how to teach is to use your right brain. Teaching reason in an intuitive manner, these professors are not required or even motivated to take a reasoned and logical approach to how students actually learn. One of the negative effects of this paradox is exposed by both Gladwell and Lehrer when they draw on the work of the neuroscientist Antonio Damasio to show what happens when we reduce our minds to the functioning of our left brains.[20]

One of Damasio's findings is that when people lose their ability to use an important part of their brain (in this case, the ventromedial cortex), they often remain highly intelligent and seem normal, but they cannot make a decision or ethical judgment. The conclusion from these studies is that even though parts of our brain play a major role in allowing us to reason and use logic, if we do not use the parts of our brain that deal with intuition, emotion, and unconscious beliefs, we turn into unethical calculation machines. In other words, the failure to nurture and recognize the role played by intuition and emotion in education can produce students who are very good at math but very bad at living an ethical life.[21]

A side effect, then, of the current push to use standardized exams to test the math and science skills of students is that we are developing only part of their brains, and we are failing to teach the importance of empathy, emotion, and intuition. Furthermore, because most large lecture classes at research universities use multiple-choice exams to grade students, these institutions often force students to take their knowledge out of context, and this helps downgrade the right part of their brains—the part that sees things in a real-world context. As McGilchrist points out, the left brain tends to focus on lifeless facts from an impersonal perspective, while the right brain relates everything to the body and the emotional experience of living.[22] It may sound as if this neuroscientist is dismissing the importance of the left brain, but he recognizes that we probably would not have math, science, language, or even democracy without the ability to abstract things from their lived context. However, he also sees that there is a great danger in basing education on only this side of the brain.

In fact, one problem with the growing trend of placing education online is that it might feed the left brain's tendency to reduce everything to a code that can be fed into a machine.[23] Without face-to-face interaction with other humans, we tend to stop using the right part of our brain, while the left part comes to dominate our perceptions and thought processes. One way of thinking about this dominance of left-brain thinking in education and modern society is that a culture based on equality ends up also stressing impersonality. For example, large lecture classes and online courses allow a large number of students to get the same education at the same time, but the classes are often taught in an impersonal and disembodied way.

As many educators have pointed out, one consequence of teaching so many students in large, impersonal classes is that students lose the ability to speak in class or even make eye contact with their teachers. According to McGilchrist, this loss of eye contact affects the right part of our brain, which uses immediate patterns of facial recognition to interpret the expectations of others in social situations.[24] Large lecture classes and online courses, then, may undermine the ability of students to develop what Daniel Goleman and others have labeled social intelligence.[25] Furthermore, as McGilchrist shows, damage to the right brain can result in feelings of depression and alienation, so the neglect of right brain functions in education may cause students to feel disconnected and withdrawn.

It is vital to realize that when educators present information as a series of isolated or sequential facts, they feed into the dominance of left-brain thinking, and they fail to activate the emotional and intuitive aspects of thought that often accompany moments of discovery and innovation.[26] This educational neglect of hard-to-quantify emotions and intuitions undermines the ability of teachers to fully engage their students and may also disrupt the process of long-term memory retrieval. Here, we find one explanation of why cramming for tests may help someone to perform well on a multiple-choice exam but may not make the person smarter. Because memory circuits often rely on integrating left-brain and right-brain functions, abstract memorization ends up being an ineffective way of learning course content. McGilchrist adds that even in mathematics, both sides of the brain are needed if we want people to learn how to use and apply numbers. He posits that although the left brain is very good at internalizing absolutes, the right brain is needed to understand relations.[27] In fact, as many educators have stressed, if we really want students to learn about math and science, we cannot just rely on rote memorization; instead, we need to teach them how to apply concepts and formulas to specific instances.

Another important finding in neuroscience that relates to how we teach students is that when people experience a loss of right-brain functions, they often cannot control their appetites, and they may engage in addictive behaviors. Because the right brain helps to integrate our minds and bodies, a disruption to these neural circuits can result in a whole host of disorders, including anorexia, binge drinking, depression, and high levels of anxiety.[28] It is important to note that these disorders are the precise problems that dominate the mental health clinics at many universities and colleges. My point here is not that large lecture classes and multiple-choice exams cause these disorders, but that failing to help students integrate the right and left parts of their brains can make them susceptible to these problems.

Some people may argue that it is not the role of university professors to care about the mental health of their students, but it is clear that psychological issues affect how and whether students learn. It is also important to stress that a lot of students do not understand their professors or have a hard time relating to their lectures because most people are unable to take a purely theoretical perspective on a topic.[29] When teachers do not pay attention to this difficulty, they often alienate their students and fail to convey the course content.

McGilchrist and other neuroscientists have shown that although the left brain is good at using and manipulating language, it is usually the right brain's role to turn language into meaning.[30] Thus, if teachers want their students to understand the value and meaning of what they are teaching, they have to appeal to the right brain's connection to the body and personal emotions. Furthermore, students should be given time to relate course content to their own lived experiences, and they need to see how knowledge works in the real world. This means that teachers cannot simply lecture about abstract information to a passive audience; rather, education usually has to be interactive and personal for it to have any real meaning or lasting effect. Some students are able to listen to a lecture and quickly relate it to their own experiences or some specific context, but many students walk out of a lecture class and cannot retain or think about the content they have just encountered. If universities really care about educating their students, they have to think about how they teach and cater to all parts of the student's brain.[31]

Although many universities and colleges claim that they seek to teach their students self-knowledge, it is hard to se how this is actually happening in most classrooms. McGilchrist points out that when people cannot use part of their right brain, they lose the ability to say "me" or "I," and to tell stories about themselves.[32] Furthermore, the right brain plays a key role in empathy and understanding others. This section of the brain develops in early childhood and helps young children to gain a sense of the social world around them. In playful interactions with parents and other family members, children learn through imitation and right-brain mirroring, and it is this type of learning that usually is not present in formal educational settings.[33]

A truly holistic approach to university education would incorporate play or some type of physical interaction into the learning of abstract concepts. Even though it may seem absurd to expect this of higher education, we do find in science labs an attempt to give students a "hands-on" learning experience. Yet most higher education simply separates the body from the mind and the emotions from reason. The result is to socialize people to take an impersonal and possibly unethical approach to knowledge and human interaction. At its most extreme, this form of education creates students who resemble autistic people who know a great deal of information but are unable to connect this knowledge to themselves or others.

In fact, McGilchrist discusses several research studies that tie autism to right-brain deficiencies.[34] To develop empathy and social understanding, children need to have what is called a "theory of mind," which simply means the ability to see the world through another person's perspective. Autistic people often lack this ability or have only a diminished form of it. In other words, unless the right and left parts of the brain are integrated, people will believe that everyone sees things the same way as they do. Therefore, the only effective way to teach students to consider the ideas and values of others is to allow them to combine right-brain intuitions with left-brain definitions. In many ways, this is a central function of art and literature.

McGilchrist points out that in many different art forms, the representation is not completed or is covered in fog or shadow. He posits that although science and math seek to represent the world in a neat and orderly way, art leaves a space for the viewer to complete the representation. In other words, art is often an interactive process that creates a dialogue between the art object and the observer, while science often seeks to turn the observer into a neutral viewer looking at a fixed and static object.[35] McGilchrist adds that in Romantic poetry, we find this same stress on incompleteness and shadow, and in many cases, these poets were rebelling against what they saw as the purely mechanical and scientific interpretation of the world that was dominating Europe at the time.

From Nussbaum's perspective, what is so threatening about the current move to stop teaching literature and art is not only that it eliminates play and imagination from education, but also that it limits our ability to think about the world of others. According to her, it is not good enough to just teach college students knowledge and logic; we also have to teach them what she calls narrative imagination, which is the ability to know what it is like to be in someone else's shoes.[36] This type of imagination can often be found in play, and Nussbaum argues that "play teaches people to be capable of living with others without control; it connects the experiences of vulnerability and surprise to curiosity and wonder, rather than to crippling anxiety."[37] I believe that this definition of play can also be applied to effective teaching and leaning. In fact, even in a research university setting, effective and engaging teachers often bring play into the classroom by showing their own vulnerability, wonder, curiosity, and surprise. Likewise, college students become engaged in and excited about learning when they are able to make an emotional connection to their education without being in a state of constant fear and anxiety.

One place where we see play in the university lecture hall is the use of humor and personal stories. Students often report that the classes they remember the best were the ones where the professor acted like a "real person." This does not mean that teachers should seek to simply entertain their students, but it does mean that a dry lecture delivered in a monotone is unlikely to engage many students. When teaching students who have grown up with constant access to the entertainment media, professors need to realize that purely written materials or spoken lectures will not reach the whole student. Thus, many professors have found that if they really want to engage their students in the material, it is important to use movie clips or music to cater to the students' different learning styles.

Although it may be hard to quantify the ability of students to think in a critical and creative fashion, we can make sure that the teachers are providing an effective learning environment. Even in science and math classes, teachers need to engage their students in an interactive process in which the application of theories and facts are disputed and analyzed. This type of teaching is increasingly important because so many of our ethical issues concern science and technology. For instance, students need to think critically about the manipulation of genes in food products and the role played by technology in extending our lives and enhancing our perceptions. Sadly, most science classes are now taught as if science is purely objective, neutral, natural, and universal. This left-brain way of teaching eliminates the right-brain aspects of empathy, intuition, and creativity. Moreover, as Nussbaum stresses, because we now live in an economy that is centered on innovation, we need to teach all students, especially science students, how to think in a creative and independent way.

One sign of understanding this need to teach the whole student is the recent move to include sections on social science and ethics in the MCAT exam required for admission to medical school.[38] This move should be applauded, but the fact that the new material will be tested on a multiple-choice exam limits the value of the innovation. These kinds of tests create the illusion that thinking merely involves selecting from among a few competing, predetermined options, and as Nussbaum points out, this method of fill-in-the bubble testing does not enhance empathy or the understanding of others. To have a truly democratic education, especially in a multicultural world, it is necessary to give each student a chance to speak and participate in an equal way, and standardized tests and large lecture classes usually make this type of education impossible.[39]

Using the Left to Understand the Right

It would be logical to expect that universities, which stress reason and science over emotion and intuition, would use empirical studies of student learning and faculty teaching to shape methods of instruction in the classroom. However, but as I have been discussing, most professors never study how to teach, and most administrators lack any knowledge about effective educational strategies. The only way to change this situation is to use recent empirical evidence concerning effective learning and teaching to shape instruction at our universities and colleges. Instead of employing intuitive guesses about the best way to teach, all instructors should be trained by using important findings from cognitive science.

As many cognitive scientists and neuroscientists have argued, a key to improving thinking is for people to be able to understand their own minds, and this form of metacognition requires not only self-reflection but also a set of concepts that one can apply to one's own understanding. In *The Hidden Brain*, Shankar Vedantam argues that although most people believe their thinking is rational and logical, their thoughts and perceptions are often shaped by unconscious intuitions and prejudices. For instance, a research study not only showed that employers will think unconsciously that an overweight applicant must be lazy and unintelligent, but if a thin applicant in a waiting room is just sitting next to an obese person, when the thin person is later interviewed, he or she will also be seen as being lazy and unmotivated.[40] This research reveals that the right part of our brain processes information through unconscious social associations, which means that it is highly susceptible to prejudices and irrational connections. If educators simply ignore these mental processes and believe that people are basically rational and logical, they will not be able to help students develop a better understanding of their own thinking or of how other people perceive the world. Thus, crucial to metacognition in education is to help people to recognize the irrational parts of their and others' thought processes.

Cognitive scientists have shown through empirical studies that most people approach reality through a set of mental prejudices and cognitive shortcuts.[41] These quick and intuitive ways of thinking save people time and allow them to sift through huge amounts of information in a split second. However, such intuitive, right-brain judgments can block the ability to learn new facts. It is therefore necessary for students to learn about their own mental shortcuts, and this can be done by first teaching students how their own minds work.[42]

People see the world through preestablished mental frames, and university educators need to take into account the fact that this is how students process new information. For example, after students learn about the ways they tend to stereotype people, educators can ask the students to write fast and anonymous descriptions of how they have seen other people use this type of cognitive shortcut. One reason to make this writing assignment anonymous is that people do not want to admit to prejudices on a conscious level, but if you find a way to access their intuitions, then you can discover their right-brain associations. Moreover, by asking students to describe what they think their peers would think, students are more likely to reflect on their own unconscious biases.[43]

Recent studies in cognitive science have shown that most people have a general theory of human nature that shapes how they interpret the social world, and these theories are often unconscious and automatic. Furthermore, although we often think of intuition and emotion as belonging to nature and evolution, this part of the unconscious is molded by social and cultural influences. In other words, cultural influences are seen as natural and inevitable because they are stored in the unconscious parts of our right brains. The only way of uncovering these automatic social interpretations through education is to allow students to explore their intuitive associations; however, this process can occur only if students first learn a vocabulary for understanding their own mental processes.

It is important to stress that the aim of this type of education is not to simply rationalize or dismiss the way our right brains process information. In fact, Gladwell demonstrates the important role that intuition and fast thinking can play in our daily lives. It turns out that the right brain is very good at looking at complex information and seeing patterns, and this helps us make difficult decisions or quickly figure out how to deal with a complicated social situation.[44] In the context of higher education, we usually ignore the part that this type of thinking plays in our mental processes by concentrating only on conscious logical and rational thinking. As Gladwell shows, the use of intuition—what he calls the "adaptive unconscious"—saves energy and time so that we can concentrate on our conscious thinking while our right brain is on autopilot.[45]

Of course, a problem with using automatic associations is that they are often wrong or superficial. For example, Gladwell discusses a study showing that students judge a professor's effectiveness by looking at just two seconds of a silent video.[46] When a researcher compared the two-second evaluations with those of students after they took a class with the professor, he found little difference in the ratings. This study could mean that people's almost instantaneous judgments of people are highly accurate.

But it could also mean that we tend not to change our quickly formed first impressions of people. This finding should make professors think not only about the value of student evaluations but also about the power of static intuitions to shape how we deal with new information.

Gladwell argues that our culture often ignores the role played by automatic intuitions because our society privileges the value of slow, hard thinking.[47] In the case of university education, it is clear that the left-brain values of consciousness and reason are often celebrated, while emotions, intuitions, and the unconscious are ignored or put down. However, there is also a risk that much of the new thinking coming out of neuroscience, cognitive science, and evolutionary theory will spark a reaction against science, reason, and logic. If we follow the underlying logic of *Blink*, we conclude that we are hard-wired to make fast decisions based on intuition and instincts, and these quick judgments are often more accurate and effective than conscious reasoning. This argument can lead to the idea that we should just trust our gut, and we do not have to listen to the findings of science. In fact, there is no reason to support education or research, because these left-brain activities refuse to acknowledge that we cannot overcome our instincts and genes.

Instead, it should be clear that we need to value both our right-brain intuitions and our left-brain reasons. This type of balanced thinking would not only change how teaching is done at research universities, but it also could help to depolarize our political world, in which the Right is often pitted against the Left. Furthermore, if educators at colleges and universities really want to reach their students and help them to overcome faulty and misleading social judgments, it is necessary to teach them how people internalize social stereotypes and prejudices in an unconscious and intuitive manner. For example, many Americans believe that poor people have no one to blame for their poverty but themselves, and cognitive scientists have found that this faulty social judgment is derived from the unconscious assumption that human nature is defined by individual genes and upbringing.[48] Also, if people have internalized the ideologies of individualism and natural determinism, they will interpret all new social information through the lens of individual responsibility while rejecting the importance of any and all social causes.

Because many teachers do not think about how their students are internalizing and processing the information presented in their classes, they have not concerned themselves with why students often do not learn the intended lessons. A key, then, to developing a culture of teaching at American universities and colleges is to educate faculty members in cognitive science and the diverse models of mental functioning. We simply cannot assume that students are learning what professors are teaching, and even if some people will argue that it is up to the students to sink or swim, educators have to take a more social and scientific approach to learning and education. In fact, the learning model that is dominant in higher education today uses what cognitive scientists call an "individualistic" or "atomistic" understanding of human nature. This unconscious social theory argues that it is the isolated, individual professor's responsibility to decide how to teach, and it is the isolated, individual student who must internalize the teacher's information. This highly individualistic model ignores the fact that education is a social process that is shaped by internal and external factors.

The use of cognitive science in higher education could not only shape how students learn but also how professors teach. Yet, once again, although most of these theories have been developed at research universities, they rarely affect the teaching and learning at these institutions. One reason for this disconnect is that most professors have been trained to value individual autonomy, in the form of academic freedom, as the highest professional goal. Thus, they may not want to think about how students learn or how teachers teach because they believe that doing so might cause them to lose some of their perceived individual power. A cognitive scientist might say that professors have internalized a social frame that interprets the world through the bias of individual autonomy—and changing this bias will be hard because it is unconscious and automatic.

We cannot transform how professors teach or how students learn by simply telling them that they are not taking into account the reality of how people think; instead, we have to develop indirect methods for getting students to change their unconscious social biases. Just as politicians have to use mental frames and emotional narratives to engage citizens, educators also have to employ narrative techniques in their teaching in order to access the emotions and intuitions of their students. Therefore, to counter the cultural bias that education is a purely individualistic affair, professors and administrators have to represent education as a highly social and public matter. Unfortunately, universities are currently doing the exact opposite by proclaiming that higher education helps individuals make more money, which is why they should be willing to borrow more to pay for increased tuition. This repeated argument reinforces the idea that higher education is about individuals' pursuit of individual goals, and it fails to acknowledge the broader social and ethical foundations of universities and colleges.

In *The Political Mind*, George Lakoff argues, in relation to American politics, that we cannot simply persuade people by giving them a list of facts and statistics; rather, we must realize that people's social perceptions are shaped by "frames, prototypes, metaphors, narratives, images, and emotions."[49] In the case of getting people to support free public higher education or getting professors to change how they teach, it will be necessary to change how people perceive higher education through a host of right-brain emotions, intuitions, images, and metaphors. Thus, higher education has to be reframed as a human and civil right, which entails changing the words and images we use to talk about universities and colleges. For instance, the Occupy Education movement has argued that education should not be just for the richest 1 percent, and this type of rhetoric has pushed the general public and politicians to relate education to extreme social inequality. This movement has also stressed that students with huge loans are "indentured" students, and this metaphor makes people think about debt as a type of slavery and exploitation.

Students and activists have also taken to the Web to circulate images and videos concerning higher education issues. Perhaps the most iconic image of the current period showed a UC Davis police officer using pepper spray on students lying on the ground, apparently indifferent to those students. This video may have caught the attention of so many people because it presented an emotional metaphor for the fundamental lack of concern that universities seem to have for their students. In fact, many of the comments connected to this video asked how this officer could have acted with such indifference as the students were obviously screaming out in pain. One answer to this question was that the police were told that the students were actually outside agitators who were intent on setting up a disruptive campsite on the campus.[50] Even though the officers had ample evidence that this was not true, they did not believe their own eyes, instead seeing the students through a distorted social frame.

The indifference of the officers who were inflicting violence on students has also been seen as a metaphor for how large, impersonal universities no longer see students as individuals or citizens; instead, each student is "framed" as a private consumer of education, just another number in a large lecture class or an SAT score to add to a school's profile. To change this situation, it is clear that we need new frames and metaphors to represent higher education. It is also important to stress that the whole grading system in higher education tends to reward or punish the individual student, which means that the social aspects of education are downplayed. In order to change this social frame, we need to find ways to reward and recognize the collaborative work of the students and the teachers.

In many ways, universities are social institutions that train people to see the world through the lens of isolated individuals. One reason for this contradiction is that universities and colleges are not just institutions of learning, but they are also institutions of social sorting. Not just do only certain students get accepted into certain schools, but only certain students get the high grades that may lead to a high-paying job or acceptance into a highly ranked graduate school. Higher education thus produces social hierarchies, and these sorting mechanisms are internalized by students and faculty in an unconscious and intuitive manner. In this structure, the faculty are caught between two competing goals: they want to pursue truth through research and teaching, but they have to reward or punish students depending on their ability to perform on tests. Likewise, universities seek to serve the public, even while they fight for scarce resources and top rankings. These contradictions are often experienced on an unconscious level, and they need to be brought out into the open so that more thoughtful and aware decisions can be made.

This book has argued that in order to move beyond the tuition trap, as parents, citizens, and students, we need to demand that all public higher education be free and that universities and college make high-quality instruction a core priority. Although part of the solution is to change the way schools are rated and ranked, there also has to be a radical transformation in how teachers teach and how students learn. These changes are necessary if we are going to have a functioning democracy and an effective higher education system.

NOTES

PREFACE

1. See Gladwell, "The Order of Things."
2. One popular topic that I avoid for the most part in this book is the question of political correctness and the related issue of research in controversial areas. I argue that these topics are side issues that prevent people from seeing the real central problems facing contemporary universities.

CHAPTER 1 WHY TUITION GOES UP AND QUALITY GOES DOWN AT AMERICAN RESEARCH UNIVERSITIES

1. FinAid, "Tuition Inflation."
2. For statistics on who actually teaches classes in American universities, see American Historical Association, "Who Is Teaching in U.S. College Classrooms?"; American Association of University Professors, "Statement from the Conference on the Growing Use of Part-Time and Adjunct Faculty"; Benjamin, "Faculty Appointments"; Cox, "Study Shows Colleges' Dependence on Their Part-Time Instructors"; Gappa and Leslie, *Invisible Faculty*; National Education Association, "Part-Time Employment in Academe"; Rhoades, *Managed Professionals*; and Slaughter and Leslie, *Academic Capitalism*.
3. Studies show that as state support for higher education goes down, the cost students must pay goes up. See University of the People, "U.S. State Sponsored Tuition Rates on the Rise."
4. In "Breaking the Cost Spiral," Robert Martin and Andrew Gillen show that universities will spend as much money as they can get, and that there appears to be no relation between the cost of higher education and its quality.
5. In Richard Bradley's *Harvard Rules*, we learn that the wealthiest and costliest university in the world relies on graduate students and temporary faculty to teach many of its undergraduate courses (xxi).
6. A detailed analysis of the cost of increased administration is presented in chapter 5.
7. In *Universities in the Marketplace*, Derek Bok, the former president of Harvard University, argues that universities never have enough money because there is always another activity or project for them to pursue (9).
8. Statistics on UC per student funding can be found at University of California, "Budget News: UC Budget Myths and Facts."

9. This book concentrates on the 201 public and private research universities that the federal government considers to have a high and moderate level of research activity. These institutions enrolled 4.4 million students in 2010, and they produce almost all of the doctoral degrees in the country and a large number of bachelor degrees. For these statistics, see National Center for Education Statistics, "Digest of Education Statistics," Table 244 (http://nces .ed.gov/programs/digest/d10/tables/dt10_244.asp). For a list of the top 201 research universities, see Center for Measuring University Performance, "American Research University Data: Top 200 Institutions."

10. For his analysis of the true cost of undergraduate education, see Schwartz, "The Cost of Undergraduate Education at a Research University II."

11. By using a very different method, Nate Johnson finds that it should cost between $6,000 and $8,000 a year to educate a student at a public university ("What does a College Degree Cost?").

12. For statistics on who is doing the teaching at American universities, see American Association of University Professors, "Background Facts on Contingent Faculty."

13. Arum and Roksa, *Academically Adrift: Limited Learning on College Campuses*, 7.

14. In his analysis of what causes the increase in university costs, Schwartz shows how the emphasis on research requires an increase in administration. For more on this topic, see Schwartz, "Financing the University—Part 14."

15. This connection between the lack of quality control and the increase in costs is at the center of Robert Martin and Gillen, "Breaking the Cost Spiral."

16. For more on the academic tenure system, see Ansley and Gaventa, "Researching for Democracy and Democratizing Research"; Arden, "Is Tenure 'Obsolete'?"; Boyer, *Scholarship Reconsidered*; D. W. Breneman, "Alternatives to Tenure for the Next Generation of Academics"; and Huer, *Tenure for Socrates*.

17. Some of the recent critical assessments of college ranking guides are Gottlieb, "Cooking the School Books"; Kersten, "Grading on the Curve"; Levin, "Ignore College Ranking"; Selingo, "A Self-Published College Guide Goes Big-Time, and Educators Cry Foul"; and Sharp, "Building Reputations."

18. A breakdown of how *U.S. News & World Report* calculates its rankings can be found at: http://www.usnews.com/education/best-colleges/articles/2012/09/11/how-us-news-calculates-its-best-college-rankings/.

19. According to Doug Lederman ("'Manipulating,' Er, Influencing 'U.S. News'"), universities spend a great time of money and time manipulating their ratings and their reputations.

20. This lack of assessment in higher education is a major theme of Arum and Roksa, *Academically Adrift*.

21. In "The Old College Lie," Kevin Carey discusses ways of assessing the quality of undergraduate education and why many universities resist these methods of shared assessment.

22. U.S. News & World Report, *America's Best Colleges*, 90.

23. Statistics on class size can be found at Texas A&M, "Class Sizes."

24. For a report on how the number of full-time faculty is misreported, see Jaschik, "Calculation That Does Not Add Up."

25. The ratio of graduate to undergraduate courses taught by faculty at the University of California and other institutions can be found at University of California. "Faculty Instructional Activities."

26. These national statistics can be found in National Center for Education Statistics, "Digest of Education Statistics," Table 345 (http://nces.ed.gov/programs/digest/d10/tables/dt10_345.asp).

27. Lewin, "Report Finds Low Graduation Rates at For-Profit Colleges."

28. These national statistics can be found at National Center for Education Statistics, "The Condition of Education," Table A-45-3 (http://nces.ed.gov/programs/coe/tables/table-pgr-3.asp).

29. J. Johnson, "One Trillion Dollars."

30. Barone, "Will College Bubble Burst from Public Subsidies?"

31. For a study on how universities discount the cost of tuition for most students, see Stripling, "Slashing Prices."

32. According to Gabriel Arana, "a 2003 study by the Indianapolis-based Lumina Foundation for Education reported that from 1995 to 2000, scholarship aid to students from families making $40,000 or less increased 22 percent in 1999 dollars. At the same time, scholarship aid for students in families making $100,000 or more a year increased 145 percent" ("Merit Aid").

33. For a study on how wealth helps to determine SAT scores and educational quality, see Hunt, "UCLA's New Admission Policy Rights a Wrong."

34. Sacks, *Tearing Down the Gates*, 61.

35. Ibid., 162–63.

36. Ibid., 162.

CHAPTER 2   WHERE THE MONEY GOES IN RESEARCH UNIVERSITIES

1. Delta Cost Project, "Trends in College Spending," 22–23.

2. Ibid., 19.

3. It is important to stress here that my aim is not to discredit university research or say that faculty should only teach undergraduate students. Rather, I am arguing that universities cannot make any rational budgetary decisions if they do not have a clear sense of how they spend their money. Thus, unlike Andrew Hacker and Claudia Dreifus, who argue in their book *Higher Education?* that universities should simply spin off their research missions, I believe university research is important However, if the cost of research and graduate education is buried within the broad category of instruction, it becomes impossible to have any degree of budgetary transparency. It is also important to note that although I seek to determine the actual cost of undergraduate education and the part of professors' salaries that goes to instruction, I do not claim that professors are not doing their job if they spend much of their time outside of the undergraduate classroom. In fact, professors are simply following the incentive structure at research universities when they prioritize research over teaching. The problem, then, is to figure out how we can pay for research and graduate education without downsizing the quality of undergraduate instruction.

4. For private universities, the budgets break down in the following way: instruction, 32.9 percent; institutional support, 13.7 percent, research, 10.8 percent;

auxiliary services, 9.7 percent; academic support, 8.9 percent; hospital services, 8.5 percent; student support, 7.8 percent; independent operations, 3.7 percent; public service, 3.7 percent; aid, 0.5 percent.

5. For a breakdown of the instructional budget at the University of California, see California State Auditor, "University of California," 74.

6. JBL Associates, "Reversing Course."

7. For the number of full-time and part-time faculty teaching at American public universities, see National Center for Education Statistics, "Integrated Postsecondary Education Data System (IPEDS)" (http://nces.ed.gov/programs/digest/d11/tables/d11_264.asp). However, this study does not count graduate students as instructors.

8. For the average tuition at public universities, see Sutton, "Public College Tuitions Spike 15%, Even 30%." For average state support per student at public universities, see McPherson, Gobstein, and Shulenburger, "Forging a Foundation for the Future." For the average tuition and state support per student at research universities, see College Board, "Economic Challenges Lead to Lower Non-Tuition Revenues and Higher Prices at Colleges and Universities."

9. My estimation of the cost per section taught by graduate students is based on UC payroll data.

10. For an analysis of how many graduate students end up getting their degrees and tenure-track jobs, see Wendler et al., "The Path Forward."

11. See University of California Office of the President, "Findings from the Graduate Student Support Survey."

12. My argument here is not the graduate students or part-time faculty cannot be good teachers; my point is that hiring people not on the tenure track or without doctorates leads to the devaluing of tenure and doctoral degrees.

13. Schwartz, "The Cost of Undergraduate Education at a Research University."

14. In the first chapter, I stated that in 2009, the University of California claimed it received $7,570 from the state for each student, but this amount is only 62 percent of the state funding the university received. The university said that the remaining 38 percent went to research, community service, and special projects.

15. N. Johnson, "What Does a College Degree Cost?"

16. As I discussed with Johnson via e-mail, this calculation is highly inflated because it includes in the salary portion the cost of professors' research and graduate instruction. However, even without subtracting the time that a professor spends outside of the classroom, Johnson's total is close to Schwartz's.

17. Schwartz, "The Cost of Undergraduate Education at a Research University II."

18. University of California, "University of California Data Analysis."

19. For a discussion of universities' eliminating course requirements due to state budget cuts, see Rosenhall, "Some California University Degrees Disappear amid Budget Cuts."

20. Knight Commission on Intercollegiate Athletics, "College Sports 101."

21. Ibid. Citations removed.

22. Ibid.

23. Bok, *Universities in the Marketplace*, 35–56.

24. Ibid., 53.

25. Ibid., 49.
26. Ibid., 43.

CHAPTER 3   SHORTCHANGING INSTRUCTION AT RESEARCH UNIVERSITIES, AND WHY STUDENTS DON'T COMPLAIN

1. Martindale, "UCI Faculty."
2. Ibid.
3. Quoted in ibid.
4. Quoted in ibid.
5. Ibid.
6. Ibid.
7. University of California Office of the President, "Update on the University's 2012–13 Budget and Proposed Statewide Tax Initiatives."
8. Gardiner, "Why We Must Change," 72.
9. Bok, *Our Underachieving Colleges*, 44.
10. Ibid., 314–15.
11. Rawlings, "Why Research Universities Must Change."
12. Ibid.
13. Ibid.
14. For more on online education and PowerPoint, see chapter 8.
15. University of California, Los Angeles, Humanities Task Force, "Report of the Humanities Task Force."
16. One of the worst things about standardized tests in large university classes is that they are often coupled with a grade curve that makes an irrational system seem rational. For instance, one of the functions of many large lower-division biology and chemistry classes is to weed out students and reduce the number of those majoring in these subjects. Half of the students is these classes get a C or below, so they will be ineligible to be accepted into the major. This system leads a great number of students to hate themselves and their chosen field in their first year of higher education.

    Another upsetting aspect of the system is that, to make it impossible for students to use past tests to study for present ones, professors make the tests different each time. Eventually, the questions become harder and harder, and many of their topics are never covered in the class. Most students fail the tests, but through the curving mechanism, the grades are distributed in an even way. Thus, one student can get a 37 and receive a B, while another student gets a 33 and receives a D. One has to wonder what message this strange system sends to students. Perhaps it tells them that school, and maybe life in general, is completely random and unpredictable. After all, students report that they have no idea what their grade will be until they get the test back.
17. For an analysis of standardized tests and rote memorization, see Kohn, *The Case against Standardized Testing*.
18. For a discussion of public perceptions of higher education, see Deborah Wadsworth, "Reality or Not?"
19. Ginsberg, "Administrators Ate My Tuition."

20. The topic of large university lecture classes has been covered in the follow-ing works: Bellante, "A Summary Report on Student Performance in Mass Lec-ture Classes of Economics"; Marsh, Overall, and Kesler, "Class Size, Students' Evaluations, and Instructional Effectiveness"; McConnell and Sosin, "Some Determinants of Student Attitudes toward Large Classes"; Smith and Glass, "Meta-Analysis of Research on Class Size and Its Relationship to Attitudes and Instruction"; and D. Williams et al., "University Class Size."

21. Murray Sperber discusses this type of educational cease-fire in *Beer and Circus*.

22. For critical analyses of universities from a Left-leaning perspective, see Gappa, "Off the Tenure Track"; Graff, *Clueless in Academe*; Nelson, *Will Teach for Food*; Noble, *Digital Diploma Mills*; and Readings, *The University in Ruins*. For more con-servative critiques, see Bloom, *The Closing of the American Mind*; D'Souza, *Illiberal Education*; and Horowitz, *The Professors*.

23. Pryor et al., "The American Freshman."

24. Babcock and Marks, "Leisure College, USA.".

25. See also Arum and Roksa, *Academically Adrift*, 60.

26. Hacker and Dreifus show in *Higher Education?* how schools are now concentrat-ing on pleasing students through new amenities.

27. Arum and Roksa, *Academically Adrift*, 3 and 8.

28. Ibid., 4.

29. Ibid., 7.

30. Ibid.

31. Ibid., 9.

32. Ibid., 36.

33. Ibid., 37.

34. Ibid., 71.

35. Ibid.

36. Ibid., 75.

37. For the past ten years, I have been studying these online reviews with my stu-dents, and we have analyzed over 4,000 individual reviews.

38. National studies of student attitudes match this notion that many students are trying to do as little as possible in order to receive the highest grade attainable. See Arum and Roksa, *Academically Adrift*, 70.

39. Peter Sacks's *Generation X Goes to College* does a good job at examining many of the changes in students' attitudes toward their college education.

40. For information on the career expectations of UC students, see University of California, "Accountability Report."

CHAPTER 4   THE ROLE OF THE FACULTY AND GRADUATE STUDENTS IN CHANGING UNIVERSITIES

1. For a discussion of this contradiction, see Nelson, *Manifesto of Tenured Radical*, 3.

2. These statistics can be found at Online Phd, "The PhD's Job Crisis."

3. See Bousquet, *How the University Works*.

4. In my interviews with professors regarding the unemployment rate among recent PhDs, the professors almost always state that *their* students will get jobs.

5. Kocsis, "How Facebook, Google, and Others Use Free Labor to Save Millions."

6. For more on the academic job market, see American Association of University Professors, "Statement from the Conference on the Growing Use of Part-Time and Adjunct Faculty"; American Historical Association, "Who Is Teaching in U.S. College Classrooms?"; Benjamin, "Faculty Appointments"; Guillory, "The System of Graduate Education"; Nelson, *Will Teach for Food*; Rhoades, *Managed Professionals*; and Schell, *Gypsy Academics and Mother-Teachers: Gender, Contingent Labor, and Writing Instruction*.

7. Each year the Modern Language Association publishes a list of job openings in English and foreign languages. These lists show that most jobs are for traditional areas and not for the new areas of specialization.

8. Hacker and Dreifus, *Higher Education?*

9. Ibid., 13–15.

10. Due to the high number of applicants for every good job, we see once again how instead of competition leading to quality, the opposite happens: since there are so many candidates and variables, the selection process becomes arbitrary. Here, the free market produces a lowering of quality.

11. See Shumway, "The Star System in Literary Studies."

12. Kirp, *Shakespeare, Einstein, and the Bottom Line*, 69.

13. See Simmons, "The Death of UC Faculty Salary Scales."

14. See Hacker and Dreifus, *Higher Education?*, 51.

15. Emery, "Faculty, Governance, and Financial Crisis at the University of Florida."

16. J. Williams, *The Institution of Literature*.

17. See Kirp, *Shakespeare, Einstein, and the Bottom Line*, 87.

18. For books on the growing use of contingent faculty, see Bousquet, *How the University Works*; Donoghue, *The Last Professors*; Hacker and Dreifus, *Higher Education?*; Kirp, *Shakespeare, Einstein, and the Bottom Line*; Menand, *The Marketplace of Ideas*; Nelson, *Will Teach for Food*; and Rhoades, *Managed Professionals*.

19. For instance, in *The Last Professors*, Frank Donoghue argues that professors have virtually no power in universities today (80–81).

20. For a discussion of graduate students and employment, see Menand, *The Marketplace of Ideas* (148–51).

21. Wendler et al., "The Path Forward."

22. Ibid., 20.

23. Ibid.

24. Ibid., 17.

25. Ibid., 21.

26. Ibid., 49.

27. Ibid., 34–35.

28. Ibid., 27.

29. Ibid., 37.

CHAPTER 5   THE RISE OF THE ADMINISTRATIVE CLASS

1. In chapter 2, I discuss how the number of administrators has gone up, while the number of professors has stayed flat.

2. In *The Fall of the Faculty*, Benjamin Ginsberg describes several situations in which university administrators found that the only solution to an institutional problem is to hire more administrators.

3. Derek Bok shows in *Universities in the Marketplace* that he is well aware of all of the negative tendencies in research universities, but he finds it hard to suggest any ways of changing the system.

4. Delta Cost Project, "Trends in College Spending."

5. Ibid.

6. Greene, "Administrative Bloat at American Universities."

7. Bunsis and Witt, "Administration Costs Rise as State Support Dwindles."

8. University of California, Los Angeles, Faculty Association, "The 2007–08 UC Expense Pyramid Upside Down."

9. Schwartz, "New Data on Management Growth at UC 1991–2010."

10. Ibid.

11. Schwartz, "Financing the University—Part 13."

12. Ibid.

13. Ginsberg, "The Fall of the Faculty," 6.

14. Ibid., 7–9.

15. University of California Commission on the Future, "Final Report."

16. Ibid.

17. Ibid.

18. Ibid.

19. Ibid.

20. Ibid.

21. Ibid.

22. Ibid.

23. Ibid.

24. Ibid.

25. Schevitz and Wallack. "UC Chief Raked as New Pay Deals Are Revealed."

26. Ibid.

27. Samuels, "Where the Money Goes in the UC System."

28. For a discussion of the UC separation deals, see Schevitz and Wallack, "700 at UC Awarded $23 Million in Exit Pay."

29. Ibid.

CHAPTER 6   THE UNIVERSITY AS HEDGE FUND

1. Swensen, "Yale's Endowment Investment Strategy."

2. For a discussion of how investment losses forced private universities to cut programs, see Wee, "Endowment Losses from Harvard to Yale Force Cuts."

3. Yudof, "Letter to Chancellors."

4. For a discussion of how endowment losses at Harvard would lead to a reduction of financial aid, see Free College Blog, "Scholarships and Endowments at Risk as Economy and Investments Crash."

5. Humphreys, "Educational Endowments and the Financial Crisis."

6. Wee, "Harvard, Dartmouth Helped Deepen Crisis, Report Says."
7. Humphreys, "Educational Endowments and the Financial Crisis," 4.
8. Ibid.
9. Ibid., 44.
10. Ibid.
11. Ibid., 65.
12. Ibid., 62.
13. Ibid., 52.
14. Ibid., 51.
15. You can watch him make this argument on YouTube. See Yudof, "Santa Barbara Press Conference."
16. Meister, "They Pledged Your Tuition to Wall Street (Summary)."
17. Credit Rating Press Releases, "Moody's Assigns AA1 Rating to University of California's General Revenue Bonds 2010 Series U."
18. Ibid.
19. Bunsis, "Analysis of the Financial Condition of Rutgers University May 2011."
20. Bunsis and Bradley, "Myths on Program Elimination."
21. Ibid.
22. Bond raters are therefore a driving force behind the privatization of public universities, but they also provide important information about the real fiscal health of American universities.
23. Credit Rating Press Releases, "Moody's Assigns AA1 Rating to University of California's General Revenue Bonds 2010 Series U."
24. Ibid.
25. Ibid.

CHAPTER 7   THE HIGH COST OF RESEARCH

1. In *Our Underachieving Colleges*, Derek Bok both he sees the push to conduct research as the fundamental force that is undermining higher education and stresses the economic reliance of universities on money brought in from research projects.
2. See Hacker and Dreifus, *Higher Education?*; Kirp, *Shakespeare, Einstein, and the Bottom Line*; and Washburn, *University, Inc.*
3. Some recent books that cover the corporatization of the university are Randy Martin, *Chalk Lines*; Nelson, *Will Teach for Food*; Slaughter and Leslie. *Academic Capitalism*; Soley, *Leasing the Ivory Tower*; and White et al., *Campus, Inc.*
4. See Bok, *Universities in the Marketplace*; Kirp, *Shakespeare, Einstein, and the Bottom Line*; Newfield, *Unmaking the Public University*; and Washburn, *University, Inc.*
5. See Menand, *The Marketplace of Ideas*, 122–23.
6. As I point out in chapters 1 and 2, most public universities receive state funds based on the number of students in relation to the number and salary of the professors. In this system it does not matter if the professors do not teach the students, and so states end up paying for researchers.
7. For a critical analysis of the research and instruction funding system, see Schwartz, "Who Pays the Hidden Cost of University Research?"

8. For an analysis of this issue, see Newfield, *Unmaking the Public University*, 210–14.

9. For a discussion of the indirect costs of grants, see ibid.

10. For a calculation of how the humanities subsidize the sciences, see Watson, "Bottom Line Shows Humanities Really Do Make Money."

11. The University of California has sometimes argued that it loses money on research grants. See Asimov, "UC."

12. University administrators constantly claim that the sciences bring money in and the humanities lose money, but these claims are never backed up by proof.

13. Yudof made this argument at a press conference available on YouTube ("Santa Barbara Press Conference").

14. For a discussion of the UC furlough plan, see University of California, "Budget News: Employee Furloughs."

15. See Washburn, *University, Inc.*, 62, 74, 75.

16. See ibid. and Kirp, *Shakespeare, Einstein, and the Bottom Line*.

17. See Hacker and Dreifus, *Higher Education?*, 82–87.

18. Washburn, "Big Oil Goes to College," 2.

19. Ibid.

20. Ibid.

21. Ibid., 12.

22. Ibid.

23. Ibid., 193, note 30.

24. Hacker and Dreifus take the extreme view that research outside of the sciences is essentially worthless (Hacker and Dreifus, *Higher Education?*).

25. See Kirp, *Shakespeare, Einstein, and the Bottom Line*, 69.

CHAPTER 8   TECHNOLOGY TO THE RESCUE?

1. See Noble, *Digital Diploma Mills*, 103.

2. For an analysis of the negative effects of multitasking, see Miller, "Multi-Tasking."

3. One of the central themes of my book *New Media, Cultural Studies, and Critical Theory after Postmodernism* is that new communication technologies are rewiring the ways we think, write, communicate, and work.

4. One of the books celebrating the use of computers in higher education without questioning some of the negative effects is Anya Kamenetz's *DIY U*.

5. An extreme example of the promotion of online education for universities can be found in Taylor, *Crisis on Campus*.

6. Moreover, I discovered that students often give their clickers to each other if they are going to miss class.

7. For a discussion of some successful and unsuccessful use of computers at universities, see Walsh, *Unlocking the Gates*.

8. For a detailed discussion of this grant, see Samuels, *Integrating Hypertextual Subjects*, 34–35.

9. One of the problems with so many books about higher education and technology is that they tend to idealize students and neglect some of their more disturbing habits.

10. For a classic critique of PowerPoint, see Tufte's "PowerPoint Is Evil." The heading for this section comes from Tufte's subtitle: "Power Corrupts; PowerPoint Corrupts Absolutely."

11. *5 Eyewitness News* presented a criticism of costly computer labs, available at Freedom Foundation of Minnesota, "Critics Say Millions of Tax Dollars Wasted on Computer Labs."

12. See Selwyn, "The Use of Computer Technology in University Teaching and Learning."

13. I thought my luck in the computer lab was changing when a new staff director was brought in, and I was asked to help design a new, fully wired classroom. After spending a great deal of time going to meetings and discussing how to make the new room effective for learning and teaching, I was told that our plans had been scrapped because the room was only big enough for sixteen students, and my classes always had at least twenty students. I then asked if I could just use my old computer lab, and I was informed that the computers in that room had been given to a professor so his graduate students could complete a research project. That was the final straw, and I never taught in a computer lab again.

    However, the story does not end there. I decided that I would use a regular classroom and just hook a computer up to the overhead projector, but I was told that my program would be charged a special media fee for each time I used the technology. On the one hand, the university was pushing for the use of new technology in the classroom, but on the other hand, it was charging departments for the use of that technology. In the decentralized university, one administrator gives grants for people to use new technology in the classroom, while another administrator penalizes faculty for employing technology in their courses. This conflict is evidence of the fact that at large research universities, no one is really in charge, and policies often work at cross-purposes.

14. Greville Rumble, "The Costs and Costing of Online Learning," http://php.auburn.edu/outreach/dl/pdfs/Costs_and_Costing_of_Networked_Learning.pdf.

15. Ibid.

16. Ibid.

17. Ibid.

18. Ibid.

19. National Research Council, *Preparing for the Revolution*, 24.

20. Ibid.

21. Ibid., 7.

22. Ibid., 25–26.

23. Ibid., 26.

24. Ibid., 41.

25. University of California Commission on the Future, "Final Report."

26. For more on the failure of UC to secure a loan to support its online program, see Keller, "Reversing Course, U. of California to Borrow Millions for Online Classes."

27. Tam, "Forum Discusses Logistics of Online Education."

28. Noble, *Digital Diploma Mills*, 34.
29. Sperber, *Beer and Circus*, 135–48.

CHAPTER 9   MAKING ALL PUBLIC HIGHER EDUCATION FREE

1. Sahlberg, *Finnish Lessons*.
2. National Center for Education Statistics, "Integrated Postsecondary Education Data System (IPEDS)," 2008, 2009, 2008–09 Winter 2009–10, Spring 2009, and Fall 2009 (http://nces.ed.gov/pubs2011/2011015_3a.pdf).
3. National Center for Education Statistics, "Digest of Education Statistics," Table 345 (http://nces.ed.gov/fastfacts/display.asp?id=76).
4. For statistics on Pell grants, see Baum and McPherson, "Pell Grants vs. Tuition Tax Credits." For state spending on higher education, see Lederman, "State Support Slumps Again." For financial aid for universities and colleges, see "State Support for Student Aid 2009–10." For federal support for student loans, see US Department of Education. "Student Loans Overview."
5. In the case of funding graduate students, I propose that we stop the current model of forcing graduate students to teach undergraduate courses and sections and that each graduate student be fully supported by a mixture of state and federal funds. This would require reducing the number of graduate students, but it would increase the number who graduate in a timely fashion. Due to their need to teach while they are pursing their degrees, many graduate students in the humanities and the social sciences never get their degrees, and many of the ones who do take ten years to earn their doctorates. Moreover, after receiving their PhDs, the majority of the students in the humanities and the social sciences end up either unemployed or underemployed. If we used current federal research funds and state support and limited enrollments, we could make all public graduate education free.
6. Burd, "Moving on Up."
7. Ibid.
8. The federal tax breaks for higher education are itemized at Subsidy Scope, "Tax Expenditures in the Education Sector."
9. For statistics on how many Pell grants for-profits colleges are using, see Fuller, "For-Profits Hit Hardest by End of Year-Round Pell Grant Program."
10. For a list of many of the tax breaks for higher education in individual states, see FinAid, "State Tax Deductions for 529 Contributions."
11. For the New York tuition tax deduction information, see New York State Higher Education Services Corporation, "NYS College Tuition Tax Credit/Deduction."
12. Wikinvest, "529 Plan." For more on 529 plans, see FinAid, "Section 529 Plans."
13. US Department of the Treasury, "An Analysis of Section 529 College Savings and Prepaid Tuition Plans."
14. Ibid.
15. Quoted in Vindex, *So It Was Written*, 52.
16. Jefferson, *Report of the Commissioners for the University of Virginia*.
17. See Pickett and Wilkerson, *The Spirit Level*.

18. See Bousquet, *How the University Works.*

19. In the UC system, after six years of service, non-tenure-track lecturers are eligible for continuing appointments, which offers strong protections against arbitrary dismissals.

20. For a call to give tenure to university instructors, see G. Bradley, "Instructor Tenure Proposals." Another possible solution is to provide instructors with long-term contracts that have a very good "just cause" dismissal process. At the University of California, over three thousand lecturers already have this type of job, but it is protected by a very good contract, and the system needs constant monitoring and enforcement.

21. The reason why it is so important to stress student credit hours is that this statistic takes into account both the size of the classes and the unit value of each class. Just using the number of courses taught by each faculty member does not tell you if the courses being counted consist of only one student in an independent study project.

22. For a good discussion on how external rewards undermine student motivation, see Bronson and Merryman, *Nurture Shock.*

23. For an analysis of defining the quality of higher education, see Wadsworth, "Reality or Not?"

CHAPTER 10 EDUCATING STUDENTS FOR
A MULTICULTURAL DEMOCRACY

1. Sahlberg, *Finnish Lessons*, 5.

2. Ibid, 1.

3. Gardner, *Frames of Mind.*

4. Sahlberg, *Finnish Lessons*, 10.

5. Ibid., 23.

6. Ibid., 31.

7. Ibid., 34.

8. For a good analysis of the negative effects of school reform on K–12 education, see Ravitch, *The Death and Life of the Great American School.*

9. For the UC union contract with lecturers, see University Council—American Federation of Teachers, "Unit 18."

10. For a discussion of Harvard's attempt to improve instruction though videotaping faculty, see Myers, "Videotaping."

11. Sahlberg, *Finnish Lessons*, 7.

12. Basu and Fain, "Performance Pay for College Faculty."

13. Nussbaum, *Not for Profit*, 2.

14. Ibid., 48.

15. For an analysis of how conservatives and liberals use different parts of their brains, see Jimenez, *Red Genes, Blue Genes.* It is important to note that most parts of brain are connected and in constant communication. Thus, our brains do not really have what some people refer to as a left or right brain; rather, there are certain tendencies that dominate certain areas of our brain.

16. See Gladwell, *Blink*; Thaler and Sunstein, *Nudge*; Lehrer, *How We Decide*.
17. McGilchrist, *The Master and His Emissary*, 49.
18. In *The Political Mind*, George Lakoff argues that liberal politicians use only reason in their arguments, while conservatives are much better at appealing to our emotions.
19. McGilchrist, *The Master and His Emissary*, 184.
20. See Damasio, *Descartes' Error*. See also Gladwell, *Blink*; Lehrer, *How We Decide*.
21. This theory provides an insight into the role of our brightest math students in developing the financial instruments that almost brought down the entire global economy in 2008.
22. McGilchrist, *The Master and His Emissary*, 55.
23. Ibid.
24. Ibid., 59.
25. Goleman, *Social Intelligence*.
26. McGilchrist, *The Master and His Emissary*, 63.
27. Ibid., 66.
28. Ibid., 69.
29. See Rose, *Lives on the Boundary*.
30. McGilchrist, *The Master and His Emissary*, 70.
31. If part of higher education is to teach students how to be critical of false information or unreliable speakers, then it is important to engage the right part of the students' brains. Studies of people with brain injuries have shown that patients with a major impairment in parts of the right brain cannot tell if someone is lying or telling the truth. McGilchrist explains this by arguing that the left brain concentrates on abstract thinking and internal logic, so it perceives nothing as misleading because every representation is part of a self-consistent system (ibid., 71). When people want to know if someone is lying, they look at that person's bodily movements and facial expressions. In fact, when people look at someone's mouth, they usually take it for granted that the words the person speaks are truthful; when they look at someone's eyes instead, they are often able to detect on an unconscious level whether the person is telling the truth. Unfortunately, most lecture classes are purely verbal or use printed material, which undermines the ability of students to connect bodily and cognitive circuits, and the result is that information may be internalized in an uncritical way—or not internalized at all.
32. Ibid., 87.
33. Ibid., 88.
34. Ibid., 57–58.
35. Ibid., 369.
36. Nussbaum, *Not for Profit*, 95.
37. Ibid., 101.
38. Chen, "A Better Medical School Admissions Test."
39. Nussbaum, *Not for Profit*, 55.
40. Vedantam, *The Hidden Brain*, 17.

41. Ibid., 19.
42. In his review of several studies dealing with prejudice and politics, Vedantam found that many conservative people do not support welfare or other public policies because they associate aid, crime, and laziness with people of color (ibid., 202). In some of these experiments, researchers showed subjects a picture of a black person and then asked them to quickly list the qualities they associate with the person of color. The findings show that when people are forced to make fast judgments about others, they often tend to rely on unconscious, stereotypical associations. Although it is hard to overcome these connections through conscious education, people can learn to monitor the way they are influenced by right-brain connections. In terms of higher education, these studies show us that if we are really serious about educating people in a multicultural democracy, we have to teach them how to examine their own mental shortcuts.
43. I discuss this educational method in *Teaching the Rhetoric of Resistance*.
44. Gladwell, *Blink*, 9.
45. Ibid., 12.
46. Ibid., 12–13.
47. Ibid., 13.
48. See Levy and Dweck, "Trait- versus Process-Focused Social Judgment"; Henry et al., "Hate Welfare but Help the Poor."
49. Lakoff, *The Political Mind*, 15.
50. For an analysis of what wrong at UC Davis, see Reynoso Task Force, "UC Davis November 18, 2011 'Pepper Spray Incident' Task Force Report."

WORKS CITED

American Association of University Professors. "Background Facts on Contingent Faculty." Washington: American Association of University Professors. http://www.aaup.org/AAUP/issues/contingent/contingentfacts.htm.

———. "Statement from the Conference on the Growing Use of Part-Time and Adjunct Faculty." Washington: American Association of University Professors. http://www.aaup.org/AAUP/issues/contingent/conferencestatement.htm.

American Historical Association. "Who Is Teaching in U.S. College Classrooms? A Collaborative Study of Undergraduate Faculty." Washington, DC: American Historical Association, Fall 1999. http://www.historians.org/caw/.

Ansley, R., and J. Gaventa. "Researching for Democracy and Democratizing Research." *Change* 29, no. 1 (1997): 46–53.

Arana, Gabriel. "Merit Aid: Higher Education Subsidies for the Privileged?" *American Prospect*, July 31, 2009. http://prospect.org/article/merit-aid-higher-education -subsidies-privileged.

Arden, Eugene. "Is Tenure 'Obsolete'?" *Academe*, January–February 1995, 38–39.

Arum, Richard, and Josipa Roksa. *Academically Adrift: Limited Learning on College Campuses.* Chicago: University of Chicago Press, 2011.

Asimov, Nanette. "UC: Millions Lost in Research Costs from Grants." *San Francisco Chronicle*, June 16, 2010. http://www.sfgate.com/education/article/UC-Millions -lost-in-research-costs-from-grants-3185121.php.

Babcock, Philip, and Mindy Marks. "Leisure College, USA: The Decline in Student Study Time." Washington: American Enterprise Institute, August 2010. http://www.econ.ucsb.edu/~babcock/LeisureCollege2.pdf.

Barone, Michael. "Will College Bubble Burst from Public Subsidies?" *National Review*, July 21, 2011. http://www.nationalreview.com/articles/272352/will-college -bubble-burst-public-subsidies-michael-barone.

Basu, Kaustuv, and Paul Fain. "Performance Pay for College Faculty." *Inside Higher Ed*, April 5, 2012. http://www.insidehighered.com/news/2012/04/05/faculty-bonus -pay-linked-student-success-city-colleges-chicago.

Baum, Sandy, and Michael McPherson. "Pell Grants vs. Tuition Tax Credits." *Chronicle of Higher Education*, October 28, 2011. http://chronicle.com/blogs/innovations/pell-grants-vs-tuition-tax-credits/30663.

Bellante, Don. M. "A Summary Report on Student Performance in Mass Lecture Classes of Economics." *Journal of Economic Education* 4, no. 1 (1972): 53–54.

Benjamin, Ernst. "Faculty Appointments: An Overview of the Data." Background paper prepared for the Conference on the Growing Use of Part-Time and Adjunct Faculty, Washington, DC, September 26–28, 1997.

Bloom, Allan. *The Closing of the American Mind.* New York: Simon and Schuster, 1987.

Bok, Derek. *Our Underachieving Colleges.* Princeton: Princeton University Press, 2006.

———. *Universities in the Marketplace.* Princeton: Princeton University Press, 2003.

Bousquet, Marc. *How the University Works.* New York: New York University Press, 2008.

Boyer, Ernest L. *Scholarship Reconsidered: Priorities of the Professoriate.* Princeton: Princeton University Press, 1990.

Bradley, Gwendolyn. "Instructor Tenure Proposals." *Academe Online,* November–December 2008. http://www.aaup.org/AAUP/pubsres/academe/2008/ND/nb/nb1.htm.

Bradley, Richard. *Harvard Rules: The Struggle for the Soul of the World's Most Powerful University.* New York: HarperCollins, 2005.

Breneman, D. W. "Alternatives to Tenure for the Next Generation of Academics." Washington: American Association for Higher Education, 1997.

Bronson, Po, and Ashley Merryman. *Nurture Shock.* New York: Twelve, 2011.

Bunsis, Howard. "Analysis of the Financial Condition of Rutgers University May 2011." http://www.rutgersaaup.org/financial/Rutgers_financial_analysis_May2011.pdf.

———, and Gwendolyn Bradley. "Myths on Program Elimination." *Inside Higher Ed,* March 31, 2011. http://www.insidehighered.com/views/2011/03/31/essay_on_elimination_of_programs_at_colleges.

———, and David Witt. "Administration Costs Rise as State Support Dwindles: AAUP-CBC's Response to the Goldwater Institute's Report." Washington: American Association of University Professors. http://www.aaup.org/AAUP/newsroom/highlightsarchive/2010/goldwaterreport.htm.

Burd, Stephen. "Moving on Up: How Tuition Tax Breaks Increasingly Favor the Upper Middle Class." April 19, 2012. http://www.educationsector.org/sites/default/files/publications/TaxCredit_CYCT_RELEASED.pdf.

California State Auditor. "University of California: Although the University Maintains Extensive Financial Records, It Should Provide Additional Information to Improve Public Understanding of Its Operations." Sacramento: California State Auditor, July 2011. http://www.bsa.ca.gov/pdfs/reports/2010-105.pdf.

Carey, Kevin. "The Old College Lie." *Democracy* (Winter 2010). http://www.democracyjournal.org/15/6722.php?page=all.

Center for Measuring University Performance. "American Research University Data: Top 200 Institutions." Tempe, AZ: Center for Measuring University Performance. http://mup.asu.edu/research_data.html.

Chen, Pauline W. "A Better Medical School Admissions Test." *New York Times,* May 5, 2011. http://well.blogs.nytimes.com/2011/05/05/a-better-medical-school-admissions-test.

College Board. "Economic Challenges Lead to Lower Non-Tuition Revenues and Higher Prices at Colleges and Universities." New York: College Board, October 20, 2009. http://www.collegeboard.com/press/releases/208962.html.

Cox, Ana Marie. "Study Shows Colleges' Dependence on Their Part-Time Instructors." *Chronicle of Higher Education*, December 1, 2000.

Credit Rating Press Releases. "Moody's Assigns AA1 Rating to University of California's General Revenue Bonds 2010 Series U; University's Other Ratings Affirmed with Stable Outlook." http://www.bondsonline.com/print/Todays_Market/Credit_Rating_News_.php?DA=view&RID=8093.

Damasio, Antonio. *Descartes' Error*. New York: HarperCollins, 1995.

Delta Cost Project. "Trends in College Spending: Where Does the Money Come From? Where Does It Go?" Washington: Delta Cost Project, 2009. www.deltacostproject.org /resources/pdf/trends_in_spending-report.pdf.

Donoghue, Frank. *The Last Professors: The Corporate University and the Fate of the Humanities*. New York: Fordham University Press, 2008.

D'Souza, Dinesh. *Illiberal Education: The Politics of Race and Sex on Campus*. New York: Free Press, 1991.

Emery, Kim. "Faculty, Governance, and Financial Crisis at the University of Florida." *Academe Online*, November–December 2009. http://www.aaup.org/AAUP/pubsres/academe/2009/ND/Feat/emer.htm.

FinAid. "Section 529 Plans." http://www.finaid.org/savings/529plans.phtml.

———. "State Tax Deductions for 529 Contributions." http://www.finaid.org/savings/state529deductions.phtml.

———. "Tuition Inflation." http://www.finaid.org/savings/tuition-inflation.phtml.

Free College Blog. "Scholarships and Endowments at Risk as Economy and Investments Crash." http://freecollegeblog.com/financial-aid/scholarships-economy-crash/.

Freedom Foundation of Minnesota. "Critics Say Millions of Tax Dollars Wasted on Computer Labs." http://freedomfoundationofminnesota.com/kstp-critics-say-millions-of-tax-dollars-wasted-on-computer-labs.

Fuller, Andrea. "For-Profits Hit Hardest by End of Year-Round Pell Grant Program." *Chronicle of Higher Education*, June 29, 2011.

Gappa, Judith M. "Off the Tenure Track: Six Models for Full-Time Nontenurable Appointments." Washington: American Association for Higher Education, 1996.

———, and David W. Leslie. *The Invisible Faculty: Improving the Status of Part-Timers in Higher Education*. San Francisco: Jossey-Bass, 1993.

Gardiner, Lion F. "Why We Must Change: The Research Evidence." *NEA Higher Education Journal* 121 (Spring 1998): 71–88.

Gardner, Howard. *Frames of Mind: Theory of Multiple Intelligences*. New York: Basic, 1993.

Ginsberg, Benjamin. "Administrators Ate My Tuition." *Washington Monthly*, September–October 2011. http://www.washingtonmonthly.com/magazine/septemberoctober_2011/features/administrators_ate_my_tuition031641.php?page=all&print=true.

———. *The Fall of the Faculty*. New York: Oxford University Press, 2011.

Gladwell, Malcolm. *Blink: The Power of Thinking without Thinking*. New York: Back Bay, 2007.

_____. "The Order of Things: What College Rankings Really Tell Us." *New Yorker*, February 14, 2011, 68–75.

Goleman, Daniel. *Social Intelligence*. New York: Bantam, 2006.

Gottlieb, Bruce. "Cooking the School Books: How *US News* Cheats in Picking Its 'Best American Colleges.'" *Slate*, September 1, 1999. http://slate.msn.com/crap shoot/99- 08–31/crapshoot.asp.

Graff, Gerald. *Clueless in Academe*. Chicago: University of Chicago Press, 1994.

Greene, Jay. "Administrative Bloat at American Universities: The Real Reason for High Costs in Higher Education." Phoenix, AZ: Goldwater Institute, August 17, 2010.

Guillory, John. "The System of Graduate Education." *PMLA* 115, no. 5 (2000): 1154–63.

Hacker, Andrew, and Claudia Dreifus. *Higher Education? How Colleges Are Wasting Our Money and Failing Our Kids—and What We Can Do about It*. New York: Times, 2010.

Henry, P. J., Christine Reyna, and Bernard Weiner. "Hate Welfare but Help the Poor: How the Attributional Content of Stereotypes Explains the Paradox of Reactions to the Destitute in America." *Journal of Applied Social Psychology* 34 (2004): 34–58.

Horowitz, David. *The Professors: The 101 Most Dangerous Academics in America*. Washington: Regnery, 2006.

Huer, J. *Tenure for Socrates: A Study in the Betrayal of the American Professor*. New York: Bergin and Garvey, 1991.

Humphreys, Joshua. "Educational Endowments and the Financial Crisis: Social Costs and Systemic Risks in the Shadow Banking System." Boston. Tellus Institute, 2010. http://www.scribd.com/doc/33964314/Tellus-Endowment-Crisis.

Hunt, Darnell. "UCLA's New Admission Policy Rights a Wrong." *Los Angeles Times*, September 7, 2008. http://www.latimes.com/news/opinion/la-oe-hunt7–2008sep07 ,0,4419624.story.

Jaschik, Scott. "Calculation That Does Not Add Up." *Inside Higher Ed*, September 14, 2009. http://www.insidehighered.com.

Jefferson, Thomas. *Report of the Commissioners for the University of Virginia*. Electronic Text Center, University of Virginia Library. http://etext.virginia.edu/toc/ modeng/public/JefRock.html.

JBL Associates. "Reversing Course: The Troubled State of Academic Staffing and a Path Forward." Washington: American Federation of Teachers. http://www.aftface.org/ storage/face/documents/reversing_course.pdf.

Jimenez, Guillermo. *Red Genes, Blue Genes*. New York: Autonomedia, 2009.

Johnson, Jenna. "One Trillion Dollars: Student Loan Debt Builds towards Yet Another Record." *Washington Post*, October 19, 2011. http://www.washingtonpost.com/ blogs/campus-overload/post/one-trillion-dollars-student-loan-debt-builds -toward-yet-another-record/2011/10/19/gIQAbUoJyL_blog.html.

Johnson, Nate. "What Does a College Degree Cost? Comparing Approaches to Measuring 'Cost per Degree.'" Washington: Delta Cost Project, May 2009. www.delta costproject.org /resources/pdf/johnson3–09_WP.pdf.

Kamenetz, Anya. *DIY U*. New York: Chelsea Green, 2010.

Keller, Josh. "Reversing Course, U. of California to Borrow Millions for Online Classes." *Chronicle of Higher Education*, April 8, 2011.

Kersten, Glenn. "Grading on the Curve: College Ratings and Rankings." *Points of Refer-ence*, January 2000.

Kirp, David. *Shakespeare, Einstein, and the Bottom Line*. Cambridge: Harvard University Press, 2003.

Knight Commission on Intercollegiate Athletics. "College Sports 101: A Primer on Money, Athletics, and Higher Education in the 21st Century." 2009. http://knight commission.org/index.php?option=com_content&view=article&id=347&Item id=89.

Kocsis, John. "How Facebook, Google, and Others Use Free Labor to Save Millions." *Wealth-lift*. http://www.wealthlift.com/blog/facebook-google-use-free-labor-save-millions/.

Kohn, Alfie. *The Case against Standardized Testing: Raising the Scores, Ruining the Schools*. New York: Heinemann, 2000.

Lakoff, George. *The Political Mind: Why You Can't Understand 21st-Century American Politics with an 18th-Century Brain*. New York: Viking, 2008.

Lederman, Doug. "'Manipulating,' Er, Influencing 'U.S. News.'" *Inside Higher Ed*, June 3, 2009. http://www.insidehighered.com/news/2009/06/03/rankings.

———. "State Support Slumps Again." *Inside Higher Ed*, January 23, 2012.http://www .insidehighered.com/news/2012/01/23/state-funds-higher-education-fell-76-2011-12.

Lehrer, Jonah. *How We Decide*. New York: Houghton Mifflin, 2009.

Levin, Shirley. "Ignore College Ranking: Become an Educated Consumer." *Washington Parent*, May 1, 2008.

Levy, Sheri R., and Carol S. Dweck. "Trait- versus Process-Focused Social Judgment." *Social Cognition* 16 (1998): 151–72.

Lewin, Tamar. "Report Finds Low Graduation Rates at For-Profit Colleges." *New York Times*, November 23, 2010. http://www.nytimes.com/2010/11/24/education/24colleges.html.

Marsh, H. W., J. U. Overall, and S. Kesler. "Class Size, Students' Evaluations, and Instruc-tional Effectiveness." *American Educational Research Journal* 16 (1979): 57–70.

Martin, Randy. *Chalk Lines: The Politics of Work in the Managed University*. Durham: Duke University Press, 1998.

Martin, Robert, and Andrew Gillen. "Breaking the Cost Spiral." *Inside Higher Ed*, August 7, 2009. http://www.insidehighered.com/node/19419/atom.xml.

Martindale, Scott. "UCI Faculty: Quality Eroding as Class Sizes Swell." *Orange County Register*, January 29, 2012. http://www.ocregister.com/articles/students-337671 -irvine-cuts.html.

McConnell, C. R., and K. Sosin. "Some Determinants of Student Attitudes toward Large Classes." *Journal of Economic Education* 15, no. 3 (1984): 181–90.

McGilchrist, Ian. *The Master and His Emissary*. New Haven: Yale University Press, 2009.

McPherson, Peter, Howard J. Gobstein, and David E. Shulenburger. "Forging a Foun-dation for the Future: Keeping Public Research Universities Strong." Washing-ton: Association of Public and Land-Grant Universities, 2010. http://www.aplu .org/NetCommunity/Document.Doc?id=2263.

Meister, Bob. "They Pledged Your Tuition to Wall Street (Summary)." http://keep californiaspromise.org/404/they-pledged-your-tuition-to-wall-street-summary/ comment-page-1.

Menand, Louis. *The Marketplace of Ideas*. New York: W. W. Norton, 2010.

Miller, Preston. "Multi-tasking: Just an Illusion?" *Psychology in the News*, March 25, 2010. http://intro2psych.wordpress.com/2010/03/25/multi-tasking-just-an-illusion/.

Myers, Jennie. "Videotaping: A Tool for Teachers." Cambridge: Derek Bok Center for Teaching and Learning, Harvard University. http://isites.harvard.edu/fs/html/icb.topic58474/videotaping.html.

National Center for Education Statistics. "The Condition of Education." Washington: US Department of Education. http://nces.ed.gov/programs/coe/.

———. "Digest of Education Statistics." Washington: US Department of Education, 2011. http://nces.ed.gov/programs/digest.

———. "Integrated Postsecondary Education Data System (IPEDS)." Washington: US Department of Education. http://nces.ed.gov/pubsearch/getpubcats.asp?sid=010.

National Education Association. "Part-Time Employment in Academe." Washington: National Education Association, January 1997. http://www.nea.org/assets/docs/HE/vol3no1.pdf.

National Research Council. *Preparing for the Revolution: Information Technology and the Future of the Research University*. Washington: National Academies Press, 2002. http://books.nap.edu/books/030908640X/html/3.html#pagetop.

Nelson, Cary. *Manifesto of a Tenured Radical*. New York: New York University Press, 1997.

———. *Will Teach for Food*. Minneapolis: University of Minnesota Press, 1997.

New York State Higher Education Services Corporation. "NYS College Tuition Tax Credit/Deduction." Washington: Higher Education Services Corporation. http://www.hesc.com/content.nsf/SFC/NYS_College_Tuition_Tax_CreditDeduction.

Newfield, Christopher. *Unmaking the Public University*. Cambridge: Harvard University Press, 2008.

Noble, David. *Digital Diploma Mills*. New York: Monthly Review, 2002.

Nussbaum, Martha. *Not for Profit*. Princeton: Princeton University Press, 2011.

Online Phd. "The PhD's Job Crisis." http://onlinephd.org/phd-job-crisis/.

Pickett, Kate, and Richard Wilkerson. *The Spirit Level*. London: Bloomsbury, 2011.

Pryor, John H., Sylvia Hurtado, Linda DeAngelo, and Laura Palucki Blake. "The American Freshman: National Norms Fall 2010." Cooperative International Research Program at the Higher Education Research Institute, University of California, Los Angeles, January 2011. http://www.heri.ucla.edu/PDFs/pubs/TFS/Norms/Monographs/TheAmericanFreshman2010.pdf.

Ravitch, Diane. *The Death and Life of the Great American School*. New York: Basic, 2010.

Rawlings, Hunter R. "Why Research Universities Must Change." *Inside Higher Ed*, March 30, 2012. http://www.insidehighered.com/views/2012/03/30/essay-research-universities-must-pay-more-attention-student-learning.

Readings, Bill. *The University in Ruins*. Cambridge: Harvard University Press, 1999.

Reynoso Task Force. "UC Davis November 18, 2011 'Pepper Spray Incident' Task Force Report." March 2012. http://reynosoreport.ucdavis.edu/reynoso-report.pdf.

Rhoades, Gary. *Managed Professionals: Unionized Faculty and Restructuring Academic Labor*. Albany: State University of New York Press, 1998.

Rose, Mike. *Lives on the Boundary: A Moving Account of the Struggles and Achievements of America's Educationally Unprepared*. Rev. ed. New York: Penguin, 2005.

Rosenhall, Laurel. "Some California University Degrees Disappear amid Budget Cuts." *Sacramento Bee*, July 9, 2011. http://www.sacbee.com/2011/07/09/3757633/some -california-university-degrees.html#storylink=cpy.

Rumble, Greville. "The Costs and Costing of Online Learning." *JALN* 5, no. 2 (2001). http://php.auburn.edu/outreach/dl/pdfs/Costs_and_Costing_of_Networked _Learning.pdf.

Sacks, Peter. *Generation X Goes to College*. Chicago: Open Court, 1996.

———. *Tearing Down the Gates*. New York: Free Press, 2009.

Sahlberg, Pasi. *Finnish Lessons*. New York: Teachers College Press, 2011.

Samuels, Robert. *Integrating Hypertextual Subjects: Computers, Composition, and Academic Labor*. Cresskill, NJ: Hampton, 2005.

———. *New Media, Cultural Studies, and Critical Theory after Postmodernism: Automodernity from Zizek to Laclau*. New York: Palgrave Macmillan, 2010.

———. *Teaching the Rhetoric of Resistance*. New York: Palgrave, 2007.

———. "Where the Money Goes in the UC System: Revisiting the Compensation Scandal." *Changing Universities*, November 29, 2009. http://changinguniversities .blogspot.com/2009/11/where-money-goes-in-uc-system.html.

Schell, Eileen E. *Gypsy Academics and Mother-Teachers: Gender, Contingent Labor, and Writing Instruction*. Portsmouth, NH: Boynton/Cook, 1998.

Schevitz, Tanya, and Todd Wallack. "700 at UC Awarded $23 Million in Exit Pay." *San Francisco Chronicle*, May 17, 2006. http://www.sfgate.com/education/article/700 -at-UC-awarded-23-million-in-exit-pay-2534856.php#page-1.

———. "UC Chief Raked as New Pay Deals Are Revealed." *San Francisco Chronicle*, May 18, 2006. http://www.sfgate.com/default/article/UC-chief-raked-as-new-pay -deals-are-revealed-2535071.php.

Schwartz, Charles. "The Cost of Undergraduate Education at a Research University." September 11, 2005. http://socrates.berkeley.edu/%7Eschwrtz/UndergradCost.html.

———. "The Cost of Undergraduate Education at a Research University II." December 18, 2005. http://socrates.berkeley.edu/~schwrtz/Cost_II.html.

———. "Financing the University—Part 13." September 30, 2007. http://socrates.berkeley .edu/~schwrtz/Part_13.html.

———. "Financing the University—Part 14." February 13, 2008. http://socrates.berkeley .edu/~schwrtz/Part_14.html.

———. "New Data on Management Growth at UC 1991–2010." March 28, 2011. http:// universityprobe.org/2011/03/new-data-on-management-growth-at-uc/.

———. "Who Pays the Hidden Cost of University Research?" *Minding the Campus*, August 9, 2010. http://www.mindingthecampus.com/originals/2010/08/ who_pays_the_hidden_cost_of_un.html.

Selingo, Jeffrey. "A Self-Published College Guide Goes Big-Time, and Educators Cry Foul." *Chronicle of Higher Education*, November 7, 1997.

Selwyn, Neil. "The Use of Computer Technology in University Teaching and Learning: A Critical Perspective." *Journal of Computer Assisted Learning* 23, no. 2 (2007): 83–94.

Sharp, William. "Building Reputations: How the Game Is Played." April 1, 2007. http://www.columbia.edu/cu/21stC/issue-1.1/vying.htm.

Shumway, David. "The Star System in Literary Studies." *PMLA* 112 (1997): 85–100.

Simmons, Daniel L. "The Death of UC Faculty Salary Scales." March 1, 2009. http://academicsenate.ucdavis.edu/pdf/the_death_of_uc_salary_scales.pdf.

Slaughter, Sheila, and Larry L. Leslie. *Academic Capitalism: Politics, Policies, and the Entrepreneurial University.* Baltimore: Johns Hopkins University Press, 1999.

Smith, Mary L., and G. V. Glass. "Meta-Analysis of Research on Class Size and Its Relationship to Attitudes and Instruction." *American Educational Research Journal* 17, no. 4 (1980): 419–33.

Soley, Lawrence. *Leasing the Ivory Tower: The Corporate Takeover of Academia.* Boston: South End, 1995.

Sperber, Murray. *Beer and Circus: How Big-Time College Sports Is Crippling Undergraduate Education.* New York: Henry Holt, 2000.

"State Support for Student Aid 2009–10." *Chronicle of Higher Education,* July 26 2010. http://chronicle.com/article/State-Support-for-Student-Aid/123680/.

Stripling, Jack. "Slashing Prices." *Inside Higher Ed,* March 31, 2010. http://www.insidehighered.com/news/2010/03/31/discounting.

Subsidy Scope. "Tax Expenditures in the Education Sector." Washington: Pew Charitable Trusts. http://subsidyscope.org/education/tax-expenditures/.

Sutton, Chavon. "Public College Tuitions Spike 15%, Even 30%." CNNMoney.com, February 24, 2010. http://money.cnn.com/2010/02/24/news/economy/public_tuition_soars/index.htm.

Swensen, David. "Yale's Endowment Investment Strategy." August 6, 2007. http://itunes.apple.com/us/itunes-u/about-yale-university/id341652942.

Tam, Jonathan. "Forum Discusses Logistics of Online Education." *Daily Californian,* November 11, 2011. http://www.dailycal.org/2011/11/18/forum-discusses-logistics-of-online-education/.

Taylor, Mark C. *Crisis on Campus.* New York: Knopf, 2010.

Texas A&M. "Class Sizes." http://www.tamu.edu/customers/oisp/course-reports/average-class-size-fall-2007.pdf.

Thaler, Richard, and Cass Sunstein. *Nudge.* New York: Penguin, 2009.

Tufte, Edward. "PowerPoint Is Evil: Power Corrupts; PowerPoint Corrupts Absolutely." *Wired,* September 2003. http://www.wired.com/wired/archive/11.09/ppt2.html.

University Council—American Federation of Teachers. "Unit 18." http://ucaft.org/content/unit-18.

University of California. "Accountability Report." Oakland: University of California, May 2009. http://www.universityofcalifornia.edu/accountability/documents/accountabilityprofile09_ucla.pdf.

———. "Budget News: Employee Furloughs." Oakland: University of California, 2009. http://budget.universityofcalifornia.edu/?page_id=87.

———. "Budget News: UC Budget Myths and Facts." Oakland: University of California, n.d. http://budget.universityofcalifornia.edu/?page_id=5.

———. "Faculty Instructional Activities: Annual Report to the Legislature." Oakland: University of California, February 2007. www.ucop.edu/planning/fia/documents/fia_annlrpt2007.pdf.

———. "University of California Data Analysis." Oakland: University of California. http://ucpay.globl.org.

University of California Commission on the Future. "Final Report." Oakland: University of California, November 2010. http://www.scribd.com/doc/44905117/University-of-California-Commission-On-The-Future-Final-Report-2010.

University of California, Los Angeles, Faculty Association. "The 2007–08 UC Expense Pyramid Upside Down." Los Angeles: University of California, Los Angeles, Faculty Association, 2008. http://www.uclafaculty.org/Admin._Growth.html.

University of California, Los Angeles, Humanities Task Force. "Report of the Humanities Task Force." Los Angeles: University of California, December 2009. http://evc.ucla.edu/reports/HumanitiesTaskForce1209.pdf.

University of California Office of the President. "Findings from the Graduate Student Support Survey: Trends in the Comparability of Graduate Student Stipends 2004 and 2007." Oakland: University of California Office of the President, November 2007. http://www.ucop.edu/sas/sfs/docs/gradsurvey_2007.pdf.

———. "Update on the University's 2012–13 Budget and Proposed Statewide Tax Initiatives." Oakland: University of California Office of the President, 2012. http://www.universityofcalifornia.edu/regents/regmeet/mar12/f9.pdf.

University of the People. "U.S. State Sponsored Tuition Rates on the Rise." 2010. http://www.uopeople.org/articles/usstatesponsored.

US Department of Education. "Student Loans Overview." http://www2.ed.gov/about/overview/budget/budget12/justifications/s-loansoverview.pdf.

US Department of the Treasury. "An Analysis of Section 529 College Savings and Prepaid Tuition Plans." Washington: US Department of the Treasury, September 9, 2009. http://www.treasury.gov/resource-center/economic-policy/Documents/09092009TreasuryReportSection529.pdf.

U.S. News & World Report. America's Best Colleges. 2009 ed. New York: U.S. News & World Report, 2010.

Vedantam, Shankar. *The Hidden Brain.* New York: Spiegal and Grau, 2010.

Vindex, Diogenes. *So It Was Written.* New York: CreateSpace, 2010.

Wadsworth, Deborah. "Reality or Not? Where the Public Stands on Higher Education Reform." In *Declining by Degrees: Higher Education at Risk,* edited by Richard H. Hersh and John Merrow, 23–38. New York: Palgrave Macmillan, 2005.

Walsh, Taylor. *Unlocking the Gates.* Princeton: Princeton University Press, 2011.

Washburn, Jennifer. "Big Oil Goes to College." Washington: Center for American Progress, October 14, 2010. http://www.americanprogress.org/issues/2010/10/big_oil.html.

———. *University, Inc.* New York: Basic, 2005.

Watson, Robert. "Bottom Line Shows Humanities Really Do Make Money." *UCLA Today,* March 23, 2010. http://www.today.ucla.edu/portal/ut/bottom-line-shows-humanities-really-155771.aspx.

Wee, Gillian. "Endowment Losses from Harvard to Yale Force Cuts." *Bloomberg*, July 22, 2009. http://www.bloomberg.com/apps/news?pid=newsarchive&sid=aQn_Cxyu99xY.

———. "Harvard, Dartmouth Helped Deepen Crisis, Report Says." *Bloomberg*, May 20, 2010. http://www.bloomberg.com/apps/news?pid=washingtonstory&sid=atKsW5.MvosE.

Wendler, Cathy, Brent Bridgeman, Fred Cline, Catherine Millett, JoAnn Rock, Nathan Bell, and Patricia McAllister. "The Path Forward: The Future of Graduate Education in the United States." Princeton, NJ: Educational Testing Service, 2010. http://www.fgereport.org/rsc/pdf/CFGE_report.pdf.

White, Geoffry D., et al., eds. *Campus, Inc.: Corporate Power in the Ivory Tower*. New York: Prometheus, 2000.

Wikinvest. "529 Plan." http://www.wikinvest.com/wiki/529_Plan.

Williams, D. D., P. F. Cook, B. Quinn, and R. P. Jensen. "University Class Size: Is Smaller Better?" *Research in Higher Education* 23, no. 3 (1985): 307–18.

Williams, Jeffrey. *The Institution of Literature*. Albany: State University of New York Press, 2002.

Yudof, Mark G. "Letter to Chancellors." Oakland: University of California, August 17, 2011. http://atyourservice.ucop.edu/news/ general/chancellors_faculty_staff _merit_increase.081711.pdf.

———. "Santa Barbara Press Conference." http://www.youtube.com/watch?v=KDVYj A4frrA.

INDEX

ABOUT THE AUTHOR

ROBERT SAMUELS is president of the University Council–American Federation of Teachers union, which represents over three thousand lecturers and librarians in the University of California system. He is a lecturer at the University of California's Los Angeles and Santa Barbara campuses. The author of the popular blog *Changing Universities*, he often writes for the *Huffington Post* on issues concerning higher education. His books include *New Media, Cultural Studies, and Critical Theory after Postmodernism; Writing Prejudices; Integrating Hypertextual Subjects; Teaching the Rhetoric of Resistance;* and *Hitchcock's Bi-Textuality.*